Why Am I Here?

(with the emphasis on 'here')

Rabbi Pete Tobias

Why Am I Here?

(with the emphasis on 'here')

Rabbi Pete Tobias

Other books by the same author

Liberal Judaism: A Judaism for the Twenty-First Century (2007)

Never Mind the Bullocks (2009)

The Secret of the £5 *Etrog* (2010)

The Question of the Hidden *Matzah* (2012)

Illustrations

Front cover photograph of the author in the BBC Radio 2 studio with thanks to Sir Terry Wogan
Other front cover photo: 2010 The Liberal Synagogue Elstree
Page 10: 2011, The Liberal Synagogue Elstree
Page 16: Creme Egg in a bush, Harrow, Middlesex (recreated in 2012, cost of egg 59p)
Page 23: aged 21, 1979, University of Southampton
Page 33: aged 27, 1984, Bromet JMI School, Oxhey, Watford
Page 38: aged 7, 1964, outside an Orthodox synagogue somewhere in North London
Page 44: Kenton United Synagogue
Page 54: aged 13, 1970, Kenton United Synagogue
Page 58: aged 15, 1973, *Kadimah* Holiday School, Chislehurst, Kent
Page 63: aged 22, 1979, en route to County Hall, Hertford
Page 82: 2009, The Liberal Synagogue Elstree
Page 94: 1995, Glasgow New Synagogue
Page 102: 2012, The Liberal Synagogue Elstree
Back cover: aged 22, 1980 HCHE Wall Hall College
Other back cover photo: aged 6, 1963

ISBN 978-1-4710-9075-2 90000

9 781471 090752

GM productions 2012

ACKNOWLEDGMENTS

A combination of events in the summer of 2011, too detailed and specific to list here, caused me to question my role as a Liberal rabbi. The Chairman of Liberal Judaism suggested that I was engaged in a bout of 'wrestling', perhaps a reference to Jacob's struggle in chapter 32 of the book of Genesis. This book is the result of that struggle.

My thanks go to all those Liberal Jews who have had to put up with me during that period of struggle, in particular members of my congregation at The Liberal Synagogue Elstree, who have probably heard most of this book in various sermons during the last eight months. Thanks too to those who were kind enough to read and offer their thoughts on it: Rabbis Charley Baginsky, Richard Jacobi and Charles Middleburgh, as well as Val Dickson, Rosita Rosenberg, Carol Savage and Alison Sieff. A special mention goes to my wife Robbie, who actually had to listen to me reading it(!), and suffer while I was working on it, and to my son Adam, in whose apartment in California most of it was written (at ridiculous hours of the night). Particular thanks are due to John Eidinow, who read several different versions as it evolved, once again guiding the process of my writing with wisdom and kindness. Without his encouragement I doubt any book of mine would ever have been published.

Thanks also to the BBC for the opportunity to share my thoughts with their radio listeners, to the presenters and their production teams who have always made me so welcome in their studios, and for their permission to reproduce a number of the radio scripts they commissioned from me in this book. In particular, my gratitude belongs to the Radio Religion team in Manchester and especially to Rosemary Foxcroft who 'discovered' me in July 2004 and guided me into the studios of BBC Radio 2. Rosemary died in January 2012, and this book is dedicated to her with fond memories of many theological conversations about the content of radio scripts and the joy of her wisdom, her support and her company.

My thanks to all who have taken the time to listen to me and hopefully to learn from me; I have listened to and learned from you, for which I am eternally grateful.

Rabbi Pete Tobias
Hertfordshire, April 2012

Rosemary Foxcroft

1944 - 2012

Listeners to Good Morning Sunday probably don't know that Aled Jones has an invisible voice, audible only to him, always speaking into his ear. It's the voice of the producer, who sits on the other side of the studio window. Good Morning Sunday has a team of producers who guide Aled through the Sunday morning maze of e-mails, texts, interviews and news bulletins. On Friday 29th January 2012 one of those producers, the wonderful and much-loved Rosemary Foxcroft, passed away, shortly after having been admitted to a hospice.

My connection with Rosemary goes back more than seven years. When I left Glasgow almost nine years ago, I left behind my involvement with BBC Radio Scotland, where I had broadcast with some frequency. I moved to London and for a year did no broadcasting at all. For a few months, I nagged my Scottish producers to put me in touch with the BBC in London and they said they had tried, but nothing happened. Then, in July 2004, Rosemary sent me an e-mail, asking to meet me. I thanked my Scottish friends for their perseverance, but they replied that they'd long since given up. To this day I don't know how Rosemary found me.

She produced my scripts for Wake up to Wogan and, once I had settled in there, introduced me to Good Morning Sunday in February 2005. It was always a delight to chat with her when she was producing on a Sunday morning, in between her words of guidance to Aled, when she spoke into his ear on the other side of the studio window.

I often heard her voice in my ear too. Not in the studio, but in countless telephone calls responding to a script I might have prepared for Terry Wogan or, latterly, Chris Evans. I have read scripts to Rosemary on trains, in airports, in shops and out in the street, and often engaged in stimulating theological discussion as a result. I cherished those conversations then and I cherish them even more now.

Rosemary won't sit on the other side of the studio window any more. Something more opaque than soundproofed glass separates her from us now. But I am sure that all who knew her and had the privilege of encountering her wisdom, her kindness and her gentleness will still be able to hear her voice. It will speak to us as it did to Aled and other radio presenters whose broadcasts she produced; inaudible to anyone else, offering calm guidance and reassurance with gentleness and with love. May her voice resound invisibly within us, may her words remain in our hearts, and may we always cherish and be comforted by our memories of Rosemary.

These words were written on hearing the news of Rosemary's death and the final paragraph was read by Aled Jones on BBC Radio 2's 'Good Morning Sunday' on 29th January 2012.

INTRODUCTION

Why am I here? A profound philosophical question? Or a rhetorical one, demanding to know what has brought us to a particular location when we would rather be somewhere else? Either way, it's a question that, I am sure, everyone has asked at some point in their lives.

It's certainly one that I have occasionally asked myself when sitting in front of a microphone in a BBC Radio 2 studio opposite Chris Evans, Aled Jones or Sir Terry Wogan. How did I get to be in this unlikely location? What did I do to deserve the chance to speak live to, so I have been assured, millions of listeners? Why might they be interested in hearing my opinions as I 'offer a faith perspective' on the news stories of a given week or invite a morning audience to 'pause for thought'?

It's an enormous privilege to have this opportunity. And it's a responsibility too: somehow I have come to be regarded as a kind of spokesman for the Jewish religion, obliged to find something in its view of the world that can connect with and be relevant to the experience of Radio 2 listeners. Drawing on aspects of my Jewish heritage, I need to entertain them, offer them words in which they can find meaning, and thoughts on which they can reflect - all in less than two minutes.

Others may also wonder why I am there. Indeed, they might ask why there is a need at all for that two-minute slot that purports to offer some religious substance to the listeners. There are those who would argue, as indeed I might have argued many years ago, that religion is a collection of archaic superstitions based on outdated views of the world that have no place in our modern lives.

It certainly does not have a right to be foisted upon those listening to a morning show being broadcast by the station known for its emphasis on 'light entertainment'. Religion may be many things, but it is rarely light or entertaining.

It could be argued that the main purpose of religion is to provide light: not in the sense of frivolity or a lack of serious intent, but rather with an emphasis on enlightenment, bringing clarity, meaning and insight to those elements of life that are mysterious or sometimes dark, lonely and frightening. The problem is that in seeking to address that responsibility, religion has shown more attention to itself than to the life it seeks to explain. The rituals it created to help shine light into those dark places have become the focus of meaning rather than a way to encourage the search for it. The symbols it introduced are perceived by many as manifestations of the divine rather than pointers towards an awareness of it. Prayer is seen as obligation rather than opportunity. Our lives are poorer as a result of religion having lost sight of its purpose. We are left with a sense that something is missing from our world: we fill it with the search for information and the acquisition of possessions, but there is no framework that allows or encourages us to search for meaning.

That certainly was my own experience of religion as I encountered it in my youth. *Why Am I Here?* tells the story of how the traditions and regulations of Judaism as they were presented to me as a young man inspired in me only contempt and disrespect. They failed completely to address the questions that concerned me in the world in which I was growing up. I suspect that this is the case for many youthful encounters with a religious heritage, whatever form it might take: ancient rules, practices and beliefs tend not to sit comfortably alongside modernity.

Religious traditions confront the challenges of modernity in different ways. The response of some believers is to take refuge in ancient certainties. Others reject their heritage completely and embrace whatever emerges to supersede or replace it. Most settle somewhere in between those two extremes. Insofar as religion is a response to the world's challenges, these - and all - responses are valid and deserve respect wherever and whenever they are sincerely embraced and practiced without belittling or negating the rights of others to observe or reject their religion as they see fit.

The purpose of this account is to chart how I moved from a rejection of practices and beliefs that seemed to have little relevance to me and my world to taking up a vocation that actively promoted the heritage they purported to represent and teach. My encounter with that heritage began in the Orthodox environment of a United Synagogue. This was one that sought to convince me that all the teachings of my faith were decreed by God and written into a book that was some three thousand years old. I found those teachings to be dogmatic, insincere and irrelevant and so abandoned them. I think that perhaps I had a sense of the significance those teachings were seeking to impart, but the way they were presented to me led me to reject them. It was only through an almost accidental encounter with the Liberal version of my heritage, unknown to me in my childhood, that I was introduced to the concept of Progressive Revelation. This is the belief that our sense of what God is and wants of us develops as we develop. A liberal approach contends that the Torah, and indeed all other religious texts, are milestones on the human journey of self-discovery, not divinely authored instructions to be obeyed for all time. They are human attempts to answer our most profound questions about our world, our lives and ourselves and to give us a glimpse of our place in the cosmos. In the end the questions they ask are more important than the answers they offer, because the answers are inevitably rooted in a given time and place, shaped by the prevailing social, economic, political, geographical and theological forces. It is the questions that are timeless, and the purpose of religion is to ask them anew in each generation.

That purpose was not communicated to me by the content and presentation of my early experience of my Jewish heritage. These displayed an approach which, rather than answering any questions I might have asked of it, or doubts I might have held, actually added to those questions and compounded those doubts.

The absence of religion from the lives of so many in our modern world suggests to me that my experience of it is not unique. Too often, perhaps, we are presented with ancient texts and told that they are truth rather than a valiant, if flawed, attempt to discover truth. Such dogmatic certainties do not sit comfortably in our twenty-first century world with its self awareness and scientific knowledge.

So it is my hope that this account of my journey away from the baffling religious experiences of my youth may echo the experiences of others, Jews and non-Jews, who have found that their search for meaning and truth was not properly addressed by whatever version of their religious heritage might have been the framework of their upbringing.

I am fortunate in many ways. Not only has my journey helped me arrive at understanding of the vital role that religion still has to play in human life, it has also provided me with the opportunity to try and disseminate that understanding to a large number of people as part of a radio broadcast. The challenge to do so in a manner that meets the BBC's requirements to be light and entertaining is one that I hope I am able to meet. The account that follows is punctuated by scripts from those broadcasts. The slot assigned to them on the Radio 2 Breakfast Show is referred to as 'Pause for Thought'. I hope that the scripts included here will, along with my story, offer just that, and I thank you for taking the time to read this account of my journey.

PT, Hertfordshire, April 2012

Why Am I Here?

(with the emphasis on 'here')

Rabbi Pete Tobias

PROLOGUE

It was another morning of biblical Hebrew. During my first year at 'Rabbi School' as my non-Jewish neighbour liked to call it, just about every morning was a morning of biblical Hebrew. Fourteen hours a week we spent learning the stuff, my two fellow students and I. They were both pretty good at it, and I spent the whole time playing catch up, struggling just to read words they were already able to translate.

Thankfully there were diversions. Conversations about the biblical stories we were using as a basis to develop our knowledge of Judaism's ancient tongue occasionally sparked excursions into agitated philosophical debate about life, the universe and whose turn it was to make the coffee (usually it was mine, as any opportunity to escape from the classroom was always welcome. Indeed, this may well have been the occasion when I deliberately cultivated the weak bladder from which I now suffer in my later years).

One such conversation, involving the teacher and my two brainy fellow students, was a confusing discussion about the difference between existentialism and ontology. My focus on their debate got lost somewhere around the word 'difference'. With a sudden flourish, the teacher picked up a piece of chalk and wrote 'Why am I here?' on the board.

'If the emphasis in this question is on "why",' he said, 'then it is an ontological question. But if the emphasis is on "I", it is an existential question.' And with a speed of response of which I am still rather proud, I chipped in from the non-academic side of the room: 'And if the emphasis is on "here", it's a geographical question.'

As well as summing up the general level of my contributions to the intellectual depth of the Leo Baeck College in the late 1980s - and getting a laugh - this comment strikes me now as being more pertinent than I had perhaps realised at the time. Why was I (t)here (with the emphasis on (t)here)? What was I, aged 28, doing on the first year of a five-year course that would lead to my becoming a rabbi? A teacher, preacher and leader of a religion that I had ridiculed and rejected for the duration of my teenage years, having walked away from it in disgust as soon as I had celebrated my *bar-mitzvah* ceremony at the age of thirteen years and one week?

Looking back a quarter of a century to that classroom banter, it occurs to me that there have been a number of occasions, or rather, places, in my life where the same question has flashed through my mind: delivering a sermon in a cathedral, leading a group of teenagers round Berlin's Jewish museum, watching a *Chanukkah* candle being lit at 10 Downing Street, sitting in front of a microphone speaking into millions of homes across the UK - 'why am I here?' Sometimes that unspoken question might have been existential or ontological, and those occasions too are worthy of consideration. Mostly, though, it was geographical: how had I, whose ambition, achieved by the age of 23, had been to teach in a primary school, ended up in these improbable places, accompanied, or rather preceded, by the even more improbable title of ‘Rabbi’?

PAUSING FOR THOUGHT

I can say for certain that one of the highlights of the rabbinic career that is the focus of this work has been the opportunity to speak on radio. I am equally certain that the invitations I have received to make such contributions are based entirely on the fact that I am a rabbi. Although my first radio experiences were with Watford Hospital Radio while I was still a teacher, I doubt that what I was offering the few patients there who listened would have been sufficient to earn me the privilege of speaking to an audience of perhaps millions on the morning shows on BBC Radio 2.

A Pause for Thought is just that - a chance to provide listeners with an anecdote or a personal experience that will give them pause for thought. And I am fortunate that my heritage offers many such stories or one-liners that are the perfect fare for these pieces.

The work that follows is punctuated by various Pauses for Thought from the last decade: some from BBC Radio Scotland, where my broadcasting career began in earnest, before I 'progressed' to BBC Radio 2. Initially these were pre-recorded pieces that were broadcast at absurd hours of the night*, but after my move to Elstree were live with Terry Wogan and Chris Evans. There is even one from Radio 4. I have more than two hundred scripts that stretch back across the years; each of them preceded and followed by informal, live conversation with whichever presenter I had the privilege to work with. That unscripted banter was often as integral a part of my 'performance' as was my prepared text; sadly it has not been possible to capture that. But I hope that the scripts, chosen as far as possible to mirror the substance of my story as it progresses, capture something of their live performance, and will offer the reader pause for thought.

* The dates of the performances of these scripts are included along with, where appropriate, the show in which they were broadcast. Where no show is listed, these were pre-recorded and broadcast on BBC Radio 2 at 3.15 am and 6.15 am on the date indicated.

My thanks to the BBC for the opportunity to have worked for them over the years and for their permission to reproduce some of my scripts in this book.

1. The emphasis on 'here'

'Surely God is in this place and I did not know it...' (Genesis 28:16)

One of the problems we face in our attempts to encounter the Divine is the fact that we are so thoroughly rooted in the 'here'. This almost always makes it difficult for us to conceive of God in any terms other than our own: religious texts are filled with God manifesting human tendencies, possessing human characteristics and even physical attributes such as limbs or a voice.

I learned many of my bible stories from a children's picture bible. It contained pages of very serious-looking cartoon characters receiving their instructions or rebukes from fluffy white clouds that spoke to them in **BOLD CAPITAL LETTERS.** Beams of light emanated from these clouds, presumably to emphasise the divine power that was concealed within or beyond them. The effect of such childhood images is, I suspect, to obscure God from human beings. Unless divine revelation comes to us in some apparently tangible form, God's presence in our lives goes largely unnoticed. The absence of such manifestations often leaves us feeling disappointed and alone, unguided, unloved, and free to behave as we wish.

My first such encounter occurred when I was about ten years old. I was a member of the 6th Harrow Cubs group and was taking part in the annual 'Bob-a-Job' week during the school holidays at Easter. In those days people could open their doors to young boys offering to clean their windows or cut their lawn without fear of being mugged on their doorsteps. I duly performed one such task for an elderly lady by washing her car. I was given my ‘bob’ to donate to the Cubs’ cause (that’s a shilling, equivalent to five pence) and a bonus of fifty per cent with the specific instruction to use it to ‘buy myself some sweets’.

I took my sixpence to the sweet shop and purchased a Cadbury’s Creme Egg (two things worthy of note here: firstly that in the mid-1960s this item of confectionery cost less than three pence, and secondly that it was only available at the time of year associated with chocolate eggs rather than year-round as is now the case). I recall walking home and enjoying my unexpected bonus when the terrible realisation dawned on me: it was the middle of the festival of Passover, and no item that did not bear a label stating that it was ‘*Kosher* for Passover’ was allowed to pass Jewish lips.

I stood rooted to the spot on the pavement in front of a privet hedge. As far as I can recall, the bush did not spontaneously burst into flame nor did big black letters appear in a cloud above me. I just stood there, waiting to be struck down as punishment for my breach of Jewish law. I even closed my eyes in anticipation of the thunderbolt or the fall into the ground that would surely open up beneath my feet.

But nothing happened. I cautiously opened my eyes and glanced around to reassure myself that I was still attached to the earth. I then hastily wrapped up the remains of the non-*kosher* Creme Egg in its coloured foil and shoved it into the depths of the hedge. With further surreptitious glances to the skies, I continued my journey home, gaining in confidence and relief with each step.

This incident raised several alarming questions in my ten year-old mind. Most specifically, I was troubled by the absence of divine punishment for my flagrant breach of Jewish dietary law. I don't know why I was so surprised. Although there was plenty of food labelled '*Kosher* for Passover' in the home to which I returned, laden with guilt, it was a place from which *kosher* meat had been absent for many years, and the family it housed was happy to eat bacon for breakfast when staying in distant hotels.

Nevertheless, God's failure to appear to me as I stood clutching that half-eaten chocolate egg remains as a significant moment in my relationship with the Divine. Part of me wanted to be admonished or punished for this transgression because the absence of divine judgment in response to my sin led me to doubt God's very existence. It certainly freed me of any sense that the Almighty was in the slightest bit interested in what I ate. It also meant that I stopped looking for God: if He (and my ten year-old image of God was certainly of a man) wasn't interested in reinforcing His own laws, then why should I bother to adhere to them?

* * * * * * * * * * * * * *

There was an incident in my childhood that I like to see as an example of how, I believe, we can still be inspired by, and receive communication from, something we might choose to call God.

It was the early 1970s. A popular trend of the day was something called clackers. These were two very heavy plastic balls on a string with a small plastic tab halfway along the string. The idea was to hold the tab and, by moving your wrist, to try to make the balls strike one another rapidly - and very loudly. A friend, whom I had met on holiday in Austria, joined me in trying to fathom the skill of clacking, and all we ended up with was very sore wrists as the heavy plastic balls struck not one another, but us.

We struggled with the problem for hours and then days: twisting the string, rotating our wrists and so on. We looked on jealously at fellow tourists and native Austrians who seemed able to produce the correct result with effortless ease. Then one day as we stood together in the middle of a field near our hotel, quite suddenly and without words, we looked at each other and each watched realisation dawn simultaneously on the other's face.

The action required to clack successfully was a movement up and down, rather than the tortured (and torturing) sideways and rotating efforts that had caused us so much pain. Thereafter, the pain was caused to others - the ears of our parents and other hotel guests - and the clackers were quickly confiscated.

To this day I have no idea where that sudden revelation came from, nor how it struck the two of us simultaneously. At the time I don't imagine I saw it as a religious experience. But something took place in that Alpine landscape between two thirteen year-old boys and some heavy plastic balls on a string. Perhaps God just got tired of watching the two of us wasting our time and smashing our wrists, so took time off from ordering the universe to send us a quick message telling us how to do it properly.

Perhaps we've all had such moments, the origin of which cannot always be properly explained: a sudden realisation of the answer to a crossword clue that's been puzzling us for days, an instant where the lyrics of a song that we have for years sung along to incorrectly suddenly emerge with crystal clarity as we listen in the car, a moment where we discover a truth that has for so long eluded us. It's unlikely that we would ascribe such moments in our lives to some kind of divine intervention - but we might struggle to find any other way adequately to describe such experiences.

(BBC Radio 2, 16th May 2002)

It was about twenty years later that I once again sought an encounter with God in the middle of a street. It was a different time of year: November, not April. The weather was different: it was raining and dark, not bright sunshine. It was a different location: Watford High Street, not Harrow View. It was a different set of circumstances: I was looking for God, not expecting Him (yes, for me in my late twenties, God was still male and probably bearded) to appear and admonish me. All in all, the situation could not have been more different.

I had just endured a troubling conversation with my father at my flat in Watford. My parents were somewhat bemused by my announcement that I intended to abandon my teaching career to train for five years to become a rabbi. They paid me a rare visit to question my decision (and possibly my sanity). I wrongly believed that my father's main concern would be the question of how I proposed to pay a mortgage and support myself on a student bursary, so I had carefully prepared a list of potential income and expenditure. (This showed, incidentally, that with a combination of tax exemption and the opportunity to teach and do youth work outside college, I would actually be better off as a full-time student than as a teacher in my fifth year of employment. It also showed how desperately the education of children was - and still is - undervalued in our society.)

My carefully prepared calculations were brushed aside as my father looked for the underlying reasons for my proposed change of career rather than its financial implications. Dismissing my description of how I saw my role in the rabbinate as a wish to be a sort of 'social worker with God', he asked me, 'So what is your understanding of God?'

That question still resonates over a quarter of a century later, and my response to being asked such a question is still punctuated with uncertainty and hesitation. I fobbed my father off with a few tentative phrases about God being all around us. Then I took the rather cowardly Jewish route of getting someone else to say it for me by showing him a prayer from the current Liberal prayerbook, *Service of the Heart*.[1] I didn't even convince myself that I had any belief in a divine power, and no doubt my father was thoroughly unimpressed.

An hour or so later, I found myself on a rain-soaked Watford High Street looking for the understanding that my father had demanded. Surrounded by darkened shop windows, I looked up to the sky with arms outstretched and challenged the heavens. 'Well?' I said, perhaps out loud. 'Do you want me to do this rabbi thing or not?'

It was nine o'clock at night, so if a message in bold capital letters had appeared on one of the many clouds that covered Hertfordshire that night, I wouldn't have been able to see it anyway. It would have required a flash of lightning at the very least. But nothing happened. And I think I'm grateful for that.

---

[1] '*Service of the Heart*', ULPS 1967. Page 93: '...dimly we have seen a vision; fitfully we have heard a voice not ours. The blazing stars, particles too small to see, the mind reaching out, the smile of children...the apprehension of mystery at the core of the plainest things—all these tell us that we are not alone. They reveal to us God, the vision that steadies and sustains us.'

Because if God had spoken to me or appeared before me, bearded and with a booming voice, no one would have believed me. Even I wouldn't have believed me. Trudging back through the rain to my flat, I think I felt as bewildered as I had after the Creme Egg incident almost two decades earlier, still baffled by God's apparent absence.

Looking back, it occurs to me now that perhaps God was in those places. When we ask those ultimate questions about our world, our lives, ourselves, in some ways we are challenging and questioning the very essence of our existence. It is the search for answers that defines us. That search is the very basis of our development, our civilisation, our humanity.

It wouldn't be much of a challenge if as soon as we asked a question, the answer popped up in the middle of a cloud in bold print or was shouted down at us from the heavens. I think God is actually in the question. The kind of question that asks for guidance, that asks for explanations, that asks for help, that asks for reasons. The real challenge, I think, is to go on asking the questions. Because as soon as we think we have found the answer, we might become complacent, self-satisfied - dogmatic even - as we cease to ask the question and seek merely to convince ourselves and others of the correctness of our answer. That is precisely the point where God becomes absent from our religion, our world and our lives.

* * * * * * * * * * * * * *

Next week is the Jewish festival of *Shavu'ot*. According to tradition, this is the occasion when my ancient ancestors arrived at the foot of Mount Sinai and God appeared to all of them in a cloud of fire and smoke, accompanied by thunder and lightning.

There are many occasions in the bible when God appears to individuals: Jacob had a dream, the prophet Jeremiah had a vision and Moses saw a burning bush. But this was an occasion - perhaps the only one - when, according to the legend, God appeared to thousands of people at once.

It can be a bit difficult trying to convince people that you've seen God. When Jeremiah had his vision, in which God told him he'd been chosen to deliver God's word to the people, Jeremiah's initial response was 'Why me?' And at the burning bush, when Moses is told to lead the Israelites out of Egypt, he protests that no one will believe him.

The prophet Elijah's encounter with the divine is almost a parody of the thunder and lightning at Mount Sinai. He too is alone when he encounters God - a God who is not in the wind, fire or earthquake that he experiences but in a still, small voice that he hears once all the sound and fury has subsided.

In the days of Elijah, Moses and Jeremiah, people claiming to have heard the voice of God would be venerated, their visions and experiences held up as proof of a divine encounter. Nowadays anyone making such a claim would probably be ridiculed or locked away.

But I believe that we all have the capacity to experience what some might call God in the way that Elijah did. We aren't likely to stumble across exploding mountains or burning bushes like my ancient ancestors did - though we might do well to stop and marvel at the awesome power of a volcano, and allow ourselves to be moved by the beautiful sunsets that are a consequence of the dust from its eruption. And when we do so, we might also hear, as did Elijah, the still, small voice of God, however we choose to define it, whispering within us, reminding us of the many wonderful things with which we are fortunate enough to be blessed every day. And if we pause for a moment to do that, who knows, maybe we too will have encountered God...

(Pause for Thought, BBC Radio 2, 14th May 2010)

Nevertheless, there were places where I think I found God, though I'm not convinced that I would have defined such experiences as divine revelation.

One moment that stands out occurred on a passenger ferry in the middle of the Mediterranean in the summer of 1976. I was travelling from Athens to Israel, a journey that requires a little explanation.

This was not the typical journey of a nineteen year-old Jewish boy to the Holy Land. These days hundreds of young Jews, of all persuasions and none, take part in organised youth tours to Israel at the age of sixteen. Many then return for a gap year, taking part in a variety of educational or social welfare projects in an environment that enables them to explore and connect with their Jewish identity.

No such idealism inspired my pilgrimage. I was still deeply resentful of and hostile to my Judaism. I went to Israel because of a girl, incidentally and inadvertently justifying my mother's refusal to allow me to have a gap year between school and university because she feared I would 'fall in love and chase someone halfway across the world'. That pretty much characterised this particular episode. A female friend had left the UK to stay on a kibbutz for a few months, so I took advantage of the summer vacation at the end of my first year at university to pay her a surprise visit. I wasn't going to do it the boring old way of flying directly to Tel Aviv. My romantic adventure involved taking a train from London to Athens, then a ferry to Haifa and various buses to the kibbutz. The journey took five days and when I arrived we discovered that there was no substance in or future to our relationship, so I made the same journey home again.

That wasn't the revelation (though I suppose that like most significant episodes in life, it did teach me something about myself). The moment came halfway between Athens and Haifa on a horribly overcrowded, dangerously aged vessel, which would surely have failed every aspect of twenty-first century health and safety legislation.

But these were the 1970s and I was surrounded by hundreds of backpackers trekking across the continent and beyond with their Inter-Rail cards (£38 for a month's travel on any train in Europe!). Like most of my fellow travellers, I had purchased the cheapest ferry ticket, which gave me access to a reclining seat (if one was to be found) or any part of the upper deck. So after failing to locate an empty seat in which to sleep, I reluctantly climbed the stairs to the upper deck.

I still recall the moment of astonishment as I reached the top of the metal stairway. I had to clutch the handrail to prevent myself from falling over or floating away, so it felt, into the vastness of the heavens that surrounded this tiny boat in a dark expanse of sea.

I had always been puzzled by a line in the Bible.[2] Actually I've been puzzled by lots of lines in the Bible, but this one came to mind at that moment. The one where God promises the

---

[2] e.g. Genesis 22:17

biblical patriarchs that their descendants will be as numerous as the grains of sand on the shore or the stars in the heavens. I got the bit about the sand, but the stars? On a clear night in North West London you could see about twenty-seven—hardly a number of descendants to get excited about.

In the middle of the Mediterranean, with no artificial light for miles around, there they all were. Millions and millions of stars that were surely numerically equivalent to the grains of sand on the shore. And that dizzying moment of amazement spoke to me of the enormity of the universe and - though I wouldn't have said so at the time - the presence of a power or a force significantly greater than any human.

I promised myself that I would revisit this awesome vision on the return journey. Sadly though, in addition to my broken heart, I also brought an unpleasant virus back with me and, having managed to find an elusive reclining seat on the Mediterranean ferry, slept right through the night-time hours of the thirty hour voyage. But the memory of that emergence from the gloom of the deck filled with hundreds of sleeping travellers into that panoramic view of the universe remained. I regard it now as a manifestation of the Divine.

* * * * * * * * * * * * * *

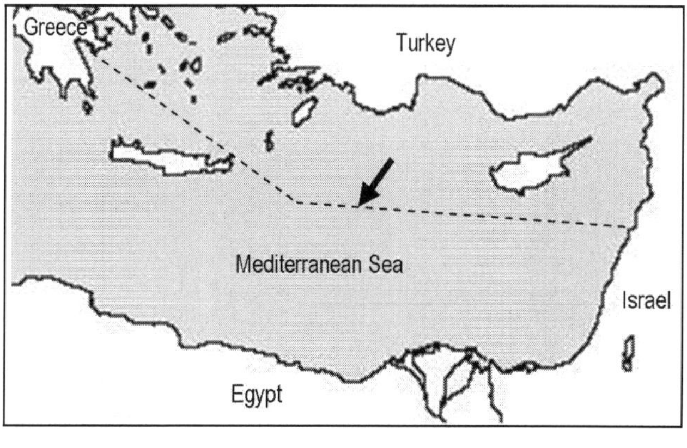

I've just returned from a rabbis' retreat where we spent much of our time considering our relationship with God. One of the questions we considered was how we don't always need special religious symbols to remind us of God. Sometimes it's possible to discover God in the most ordinary places.

One morning I couldn't find my toothpaste so I tried my wife's special toothpaste for sensitive teeth. It was truly awful: so bad that I actually exclaimed out loud. I don't think I mentioned God in my outburst, but when I opened the bathroom cabinet to return the offending substance, my missing tube of toothpaste fell straight into my hand.

I'm not suggesting that God had nothing better to do than nudge my tube of toothpaste out of its hiding place into my waiting hand - and were I to try to convince you of that, I think should be escorted from the studio and told never to return. Because I think anyone who believes that God intervenes in our lives in such a manner is destined to be disappointed. But I think God was in my thoughts that followed this extraordinary event.

If I'd found my toothpaste right away, I'd have brushed my teeth and carried on with my day without a second thought. But its absence, followed by its apparently miraculous appearance made me stop and consider other miraculous things going on around me. Water - hot and cold - flowed at the turn of a tap, light shone from the fitting above me, another day was dawning beyond the bathroom window as the earth continued its imperceptible turning. I suddenly felt acutely aware of - and grateful for - so many of the simple things we take for granted.

And now those thoughts come to my mind every time I take my toothpaste out of the bathroom cabinet. Of course I'm not worshipping the toothpaste tube. I suppose it's a kind of symbol - one that inspires me to take notice of my world. And I think it shows how even the most ordinary things can become symbols that remind us to give thanks for God's world.

(Pause for Thought, BBC Radio 2, 23rd November 2011)

Another memorable encounter took place close to that 1970s experience. I had, despite not receiving an answer to my question in Watford High Street, embarked upon a five-year training course to become a rabbi. Rabbinic students were obliged to spend the third year of the course studying in Israel and part of that study involved visiting various biblical sites to explore Jewish history.

It was September 1987, a few days before the spontaneous outburst of Palestinian fury that became known as the first *intifada*. That meant it was still possible to travel as tourists into the West Bank without (much) fear of being shot at or stoned. Our journey that day took us to Shiloh, which had been an important biblical shrine in the days of the Judges some three thousand years earlier.

The ancient shrine of Shiloh was located at the top of a hill (my ancestors had a penchant for worshipping God in high places). The coach was parked at the foot of the hill and some thirty students (mostly American) made the not too arduous ten minute climb to the summit.

There was nothing there. Some trees, a few bits of stone and rock which might once have been parts of buildings strewn around, a lot of open green space and a rusty sign in Hebrew and English which effectively stated 'The prophet Samuel was here'.

Our teacher gave a rather perfunctory summary of the role of Shiloh in ancient Israelite history and then told us to return to the bus. This invitation was gratefully accepted by most of the students as it was hot, getting towards the end of a long day, and there really was nothing to see.

Three of us remained behind, however. I felt suddenly awestruck, mesmerised by something that I couldn't begin to define. A gentle breeze was blowing and as I stood, transfixed, I felt as though it was touching me, caressing my face, whispering in my ears. It wasn't saying anything; again, had I imagined that I was hearing spoken words, I would have turned and walked away with a mixture of disbelief and self-contempt at my own gullibility. There was just something special about the place. I think the others, who stood there with me for what seemed like an age while our colleagues descended the hill, felt it too. We were yelled at when we eventually boarded the bus, but the sense of serenity and, well, something 'other' made that easy to ignore.

The following day I did some research in the library of the Hebrew Union College in Jerusalem (there was no such thing as Google back then) and discovered that Shiloh was one of the quietest places on earth because the topography of the surrounding hills made it a natural auditorium where a human voice speaking at a normal volume could be heard from several hundred feet away.

There was more than that. I think it was also a place where it was possible to hear the past, to feel a presence, to sense something mystical. I became convinced that this was a place that had surely touched others as it had touched me and I decided that my forty thousand word rabbinic thesis that would be the focus of my final year at college would be about Shiloh. Unfortunately, a few months later news of a proposed scholarly work on that very subject was announced,[3] which scuppered that idea. (Instead I focused my thesis on King Jeroboam, but that is, quite literally, another story.)

Nevertheless, I was convinced that something extraordinary must have happened at Shiloh and fantasised that it might have been home to manifestations of divine inspiration. I was delighted when further research revealed that one of the literary sources of the Hebrew scriptures, the Torah, is thought by scholars to have been created in what was the northern kingdom of Israel (for those in the know, this was the *Elohist* or 'E') and it is not unreasonable to assume that whoever wrote this material may well have been based at Shiloh.

Less than a week after I visited Shiloh with my fellow students, it was sealed off behind the line that divided Israel from the occupied Palestinian territories of the West Bank and has done so ever since. It would probably be possible, if a little dangerous, to return. I never have, perhaps out of a fear that a second visit may not match the first. I prefer to hold the unspoiled memory of what might have been an encounter with the Divine in a place

---

[3] *Shiloh: a Biblical City in Tradition and History*, Donald Schley, published in Catholic Biblical Quarterly, 1991

steeped in the history of Israelite prophecy that is at the heart of my connection to Judaism.

* * * * * * * * * * * * *

It's been several weeks since the last Jewish festival, but I'm happy to say that we've just reached another one. The festival of *Shavu'ot* - known as Pentecost - begins this evening.

In biblical times, this was the harvest of the first fruits, but the ancient rabbis of Judaism gave it extra significance by declaring that this was the occasion when the Israelites received the Ten Commandments at Mount Sinai. And so we celebrate the revealing of God's instructions to our ancestors, which have been passed down through the generations since that mysterious and awesome moment.

According to the account in the book of Exodus, the event was witnessed by all the people and was accompanied by earthquake, thunder and lightning. Many years later, when the prophet Elijah visited the same place, he too experienced God: not in fire or earthquake, but in the still small voice that spoke to him after they had passed.

I remember as a child reading a picture bible, which portrayed God as speaking to people in bold capital letters in the midst of a cloud from which emanated rays of light. I can honestly say that I've never seen - or heard - God speaking in such a manner.

But in my teaching days, I've seen a child's face light up with sudden understanding of a concept that has previously eluded them. As a rabbi I've seen marrying couples look at one another with eyes that speak of a mystical connection, and at times I've heard music or enjoyed scenery that has moved me and touched my soul.

So as I prepare to celebrate with my community this evening, I think I prefer the simplicity of Elijah's vision to the divine pyrotechnics of Mount Sinai. Whether it be a sudden understanding of long division, the joy of loving and being loved, or the recognition of beauty in our world, God's still small voice can speak to us at any time: all we have to do is listen.

(Pause for Thought, BBC Radio 2, 7th June 2011)

These memories of where I have found - or not found - God, the most recent of which is already half a lifetime ago, remind me that there are, perhaps, certain places where we are more exposed to whatever we call God, or where whatever we call God is more available to us.

Maybe that's how God works: not with blinding flashes of light, fiery bushes that are not consumed by flames or bold capital letters written on glowing clouds accompanied by booming voices. The absence of melodramatic revelatory signs does not mean the absence of God. It just means the absence of the sort of God who occupies our childhood imaginations, the one with the long white beard sitting on the cloud looking down and waiting for us to make a mistake so He can punish us. And given the way that kind of God behaves in the Hebrew Bible (which Christians call the Old Testament), we're probably better off without Him.

But what we refer to as God (for want of a better word to describe something invisible, indefinable and completely beyond our ability to comprehend) is both more obscure and more accessible than that. God is a presence, a challenge, a demand, a possibility. And the quest to feel that presence, to meet that challenge, to respond to that demand, to achieve that possibility is a religious quest, a human quest and a manifestation of the Divine. Humankind, when it aspires to fulfil its highest potential, is seeking to carry out God's will: not in the sense of performing certain ritual tasks, but in striving to become what it can become.

Occasionally I wonder whether God was present as I strove – unconsciously – to become what I would eventually become. Not as some guiding voice, which would have been literally incredible and would have sent me running in the opposite direction. It was the manner in which I followed what I believed was my chosen path and found myself heading towards a most improbable destination.

I qualified as a primary school teacher at the age of twenty-three and believed that I had found my place, with my little community of ten and eleven year-olds. After four years it had become clear to me that I was more concerned about their development and wellbeing than their ability to spell. I also found it hard to dedicate myself to a new group of children at the start of each school year. I wanted more continuity. I wanted to work with a community that was geared more towards promoting human values than learning long division, one to which I didn't have to bid farewell every July.

At the end of this fourth year of teaching, I took a holiday in the south of France, staying in the apartment of my in-laws-to-be. There was a sizeable library in the bathroom and among all the joke books and other light-hearted material, my eye was drawn to one by Harry Kemelman, entitled *Conversations with Rabbi Small*. This book, which I rescued from its inglorious and incongruous location, explained Judaism to me in a way that it had never previously been presented. It wasn't just a collection of obscure requirements and prohibitions in a strange language to which I had been required to pay homage. Rather it was a series of responses to, and ways of dealing with, life's questions and challenges. Rooted in antiquity, it provided a framework that invited and encouraged its adherents to confront those questions and challenges.

Looking back now, it seems that these were milestones on this journey I did not even know I was undertaking. Perhaps everyone's life looks like this in retrospect: a series of apparently unconnected incidents that add up to a momentous, life-changing decision. Were I to suggest that God was in each of those places, arranging events in order to shape my decision to change my employment and my employer, I would request that this book not even be given a place on the shelf where I had fortuitously found Kemelman's small volume, but put directly into the WC beneath it. The very notion of my, or anyone's, life being directed in such a way had been wrapped in foil and firmly shoved into a hedge a decade and a half earlier.

Perhaps God is a manifestation of the challenges we face on the journey towards becoming the people we have the potential to become. We can respond to those challenges and follow their apparent direction. Or we can ignore them and keep to the path we believe we have mapped out for ourselves. I could have ignored the series of events that took me to a Jewish education conference one Boxing Day:

My volunteering at a local hospital one December 25th to escape from the annual melancholy that descended on me once the primary school celebration of Christmas had, as usual, come to an end the previous week.

The fact that I travelled the short distance from that hospital to the home of a friend, who happened to be a rabbi, once my Christmas lunch serving duties were completed.

His invitation to me to leave my car at his house and accompany him the following day to assist him with a presentation at an education conference.

The enthusiasm and dedication of the forty or so teachers and educators who were there. This all impressed me so much that when we arrived back at his house that evening, I got into my car and returned to the conference, uninvited, unknown and certainly unpaid for. I left there sporting a badge stating - to my friends' amusement - 'Jewish Education Is More Important Than Anything Else'.

Was that just a collection of coincidences? Or was it a series of places in my life that added up to a challenge to engage in a search for meaning that would take me in a new direction, from the classroom to the pulpit? Whatever it was, less than two years later I was back at the rabbi's house. I had, by now, joined his congregation, and was asking him what I needed to do to become a rabbi like him. He seemed less bemused than me at the request; perhaps he had a greater understanding of what lay behind the combination of seemingly random experiences that had brought me - the unbelieving repudiator of Orthodox Judaism - to this improbable place.

The following September I was at the Leo Baeck College, commencing my studies that would lead to my becoming a rabbi. It was fifteen years since I had sat in a classroom to learn about Judaism. At the time, I could not wait to get out of that environment. Yet here I was voluntarily re-entering it, albeit in a very different context. Whatever it was that had brought me to this place, it owed little to the Judaism that had been presented to me in the classrooms and other locations of my childhood.

Having considered what might have been the external influences that had apparently guided me here, it is now time to move the emphasis from the 'here' to the 'I'.

The internal development that was a response to those influences was shaped in my home, in Orthodox synagogue services and in classrooms very different from the one in which I now found myself. Childhood encounters with religious heritage are often challenging. I hope that my story will demonstrate that lurking behind the most bewildering and negative of experiences lies the possibility of a genuine engagement with one's heritage, and glimpses of a truth that is so often concealed from those who seek it.

A recent Panorama programme talked about the criteria an organisation has to meet in order for the Charity Commission to classify it as a religion.

Many people today are alienated by religion. It's often regarded as being little more than ancient superstition. Biologist Richard Dawkins describes religion as 'dangerous nonsense' while philosopher A C Grayling condemns the belief in supernatural entities in the universe. Science, they claim, has completely superseded religion and religion should therefore be scrapped as ancient and worthless.

But I think it's important to remember what religion was in its earliest form. Thousands of years ago, our ancestors understood very little about their world. Every natural phenomenon, from illnesses to thunderstorms, filled them with dread. In every manifestation of nature, the earliest human beings saw the work of forces they could not understand. Life was a series of questions for our ancestors to unravel and seek to comprehend. And what we now call religion was their answer to those questions.

Many of the answers they came up with we now recognise as being naïve or just plain wrong. But at the time, they were the most forward-thinking ideas of their day. They sought to find meaning in a world that didn't make sense. They did so with sacrifices and rituals, rules and regulations that would be unlikely to impress the Charity Commissioners seeking to define a religion in our day and age.

But religion is also meant to give us hope. And whether it be in a wilderness three thousand years ago or on our crowded twenty-first century streets, that is also a function of religion. To offer a vision of humankind living in harmony with itself, its world and its creator. To develop an understanding not just of how our world works but why. To recognise that no one view of the world is any better than any other but that all attempts to explain and give meaning and purpose to human life are valid and important.

I don't actually know what are the Charity Commission's criteria for classifying something as a religion. But if it ticked all the boxes I've just listed, maybe religion could rid itself of the suspicion and condemnation it so often attracts and reclaim its rightful place as a force for good in the world.

(Pause for Thought, BBC Radio 2, 16th May 2007)

The emphasis on 'I'

'If I go to the Israelite people and say to them "The God of your ancestors has sent me" and they ask me "What is the name of this God?" what shall I say to them?' (Exodus 3:13)

For most young Jews, I suspect, the introduction to the mysteries of their religious heritage occurs on the Jewish New Year and Day of Atonement. Of course, for boys, there is an earlier introduction to that heritage in the form of circumcision: it is, thankfully, sufficiently early not to remain part of their conscious memory, though the possibility of some subliminal effect cannot accurately be gauged.

The effect on Jews of obligatory annual autumn visits to religious services is also difficult to measure. It involved a couple of days off school shortly after the start of a new academic year (three if you were Orthodox, two if you were Progressive, though the latter was an unknown quantity in my family). There was also the obligation to dress in smart clothes and to join fellow Jews in this annual pilgrimage to their synagogue, or to whatever location had temporarily become their synagogue, if the establishment in which regular worship took place was not large enough to contain these two- or three-day-a-year Jews.

For my family, the location of this annual encounter was a rather gloomy social hall in Kenton. My mother and sister were obliged to look down on proceedings from a balcony; my father and I were on the ground floor, surrounded by a combination of earnest worshippers chanting in Hebrew and mystified, bored boys being chastised by their equally mystified, bored fathers.

I have a vague memory of one occasion, when I was ten or eleven years old, which took place after we had returned from another mind-numbingly dull September morning at the social hall turned synagogue. For reasons unknown, I gathered together various teddy bears and other soft toys and placed them all in an armchair in the living room of my house. I then set up my own little sanctuary by draping them in my *tallit* and proceeded to sway backwards and forwards in front of them, mumbling incoherently as I did so. Presumably I was acting out what I had experienced that morning. Perhaps that was the year of the Creme Egg incident, and I felt a need for personal atonement. Whatever the reason, it was a rather bizarre precursor of what the future would hold.

Contained in the book from which I was pretending to read were prayers that had been intoned all around me earlier that morning. Had I been able to understand their content, I would have been horrified that I was assuring my inanimate congregation that God was in the process of deciding who would live and who would die by storm, by pestilence, by the sword and so on. The lengthy list of different ways in which human life could be curtailed concluded with the reminder that '...repentance, prayer and good deeds could avert the severity of the decree'.

This was scary stuff. It was probably meant to be. Its intention, I suppose, was to remind us of our vulnerability and frailty, the fragile thread from which our existence hung, and the obligation to behave in a way that would be pleasing to whatever Being had the power to break or sustain that thread. Its effect, on me at least, was to make it seem that anyone who died had clearly failed to repent properly, or had done something so heinous that they had merited the ultimate divine punishment. Perhaps the fact that these judgmental statements took place against a background of floods in Bangladesh, famine in Biafra or the disaster in Aberfan (to quote but a few examples of far, far too many places in the world of my childhood where innocent children died) made them seem more odious. But the whole notion of God writing people's names in a book between *Rosh ha-Shanah* and *Yom Kippur,* in whatever language, was so offensive that for me it rendered the entire process of High Holyday prayer and repentance absurd.

The opportunity, afforded me in future years, to attend services with my friends rather than with my father helped to relieve some of the agony but the sense of pointlessness remained. So much so that one year I encouraged a group of friends to leave a *Kol Nidre* service on the eve of *Yom Kippur* at Wembley Liberal Synagogue after a mere twenty minutes and head to the fish and chip shop next door. I don't know if he found this out, but the following year my father seemed to prefer me to be with him, so I agreed with all the good grace one would expect from a teenage boy.

Rosh ha-Shanah fell that year on a Saturday, the day of the final of the Gillette Cup, a cricket competition in which our beloved local team, whom my father and I had watched on many occasions together, were competing. The game was being broadcast live on television. It was clear that we both wanted to watch it.

I had rehearsed my speech, which would sum up all the doubts I had assembled over the years, ready to respond to my father's demand that I accompany him to synagogue. When the morning came my courage deserted me, and I remained hidden in my bedroom until after I heard the front door close. At that point I went to the bathroom where I was met by my father who had, I presume, closed the front door from within to lure me from my concealment.

"Are you coming to *shul*?" he asked.

"No," I replied, seeing my wise thoughts pass unspoken before my mind's eye.

"And why's that?" he challenged.

I thought of my theological arguments. I wanted to point out that surely he would rather watch the cricket. After a long pause, I finally managed my stammered response.

"Because I don't want to."

After all those years of religious and secular education poured into one about to head off to university, that was the best I could muster.

"Well it's good to know that you think you have all the answers at such an early age," was his sarcastic, grim-faced response. He turned, went downstairs and left the house. At least he managed to get his line out properly.

Less than three hours later he was back, and we watched the cricket together in an awkward silence. Middlesex were resoundingly thrashed by Lancashire; their performance as inadequate as mine that morning. Losers in sporting events usually console one another by looking forward to the next year. For my father and me it was not clear what the next or any future Jewish New Year would hold.

* * * * * * * * * * * * *

Just over two weeks ago, my son celebrated his bar-mitzvah ceremony. This is when a Jewish child, on reaching the age of thirteen, reads from the Torah, the holy scroll of Judaism, in the presence of the community. My son's reading was on the theme of revelation, the legend of the appearance of God at Mount Sinai over three thousand years ago. Every religion has as its origin such a moment, when heaven and earth meet one another and humanity is briefly touched by the divine.

Whatever dwells in the mystery beyond our comprehension reaches down to us at such times, and we, in ways which are equally impossible to explain, rise up to meet it. This does not just occur in powerful moments of revelation like the one experienced by the Israelites at Mount Sinai, but also in very private, personal moments in our individual lives. My son standing before the community declaring his commitment to it was one such moment. It was an occasion where heaven and earth briefly met, where I was able to step out of the everyday to a level of experience which exists on a different plane.

It was on that same plane that I felt the absence of my late father from that ceremony. Yesterday was the first anniversary of his death - known by the Yiddish word Yahrzeit. In Jewish tradition, a memorial candle which burns for 24 hours, is kindled on the anniversary of the death of a loved one. I lit the candle and left it flickering in the hallway of my house. I passed by it many times during the day and experienced a gentle sense of its warmth and light each time I acknowledged its presence. Perhaps I even engaged in a private conversation with it on occasion, I couldn't say for sure. But I know that I had a keener awareness of my father's presence - and absence - each time I glimpsed that candle.

Once again, heaven and earth had met. I cannot say for sure where my father now dwells - the mystery is too impenetrable - but I have no doubt that he was closer to me while that candle glowed in my home. And he was there also at my son's bar-mitzvah ceremony, touching this life in a way that is always possible when heaven and earth draw close to one another.

(Thought for the Day, BBC Radio Scotland, 20th February 2002)

Most of my childhood encounters with Judaism did not take place in the temporary place of worship where we annually implored God to grant us another year of life, and certainly not in my home. They happened in the building in which my *bar-mitzvah* ceremony at the age of thirteen would eventually take place. In the year or so leading up to that ceremony, I attended just about every weekly Sabbath morning service. Mostly I travelled on my own by bus; occasionally I was accompanied by my father. He would drive and park the car about half a mile away from the synagogue leaving us to walk the remaining distance.

The absurdity of using these various means of travel on a day when such actions were supposedly prohibited served only to increase my bewilderment with the religion that was apparently my heritage. Had it been explained to me that there were those for whom such regulations spoke of a commitment to an ancient covenant and that adherence to them was an expression of a sincerely held belief, I might have found some understanding of, and had some sympathy with, these rules. Instead, I was left with a series of confusing prohibitions, most of which I breached, the origin and purpose of which remained a mystery.

This confusion was heightened, rather than diminished, by the process known as religious education that took place in the same building. I have little memory of the layout of the place. I know that it had several classrooms and an ingenious set of sliding doors that turned the hall in which prayers were recited on a Sabbath into yet more rooms. I have even less memory of what went on in those rooms every Sunday morning during term time.

The memories I do retain have little to do with the content of what, presumably, I was supposed to learn. I recall my first day, at the age of five, when I spent the entire morning crying - an interesting forerunner of what would be my attitude to my heritage. I also remember that many hours of each Sunday morning were spent with a friend of similar age called Colin, organising ever more complex football tournaments, using dice that we would sneak into class and reams of paper with lists of imaginary fixtures. If we were lucky, and able to disguise the throws of the dice and the recording of the results, we might manage to complete an entire First Division season in a Sunday morning. A favourite memory is of being thrown out of the class by a teacher who wanted to introduce us to Israel. He put a map of that country on the board and informed us that Israel was about the same size as Wales. I put my hand up and asked him how many whales - and missed the rest of his introduction.

It was the encounters with the rabbi, who was unleashed upon us once we reached the age of twelve, that did the most damage to my already strained relationship with my religious heritage. At this point our exposure to this mysterious process of religious education increased to three times a week as Tuesday and Thursday evenings were added to Sunday mornings. He did praise me once, when I pleased him by keeping the scores in a quiz, only for that praise to turn to shouts of rage when he saw that I had written them in pen on my arm. Subsequent awareness of Levitical law suggested to me that this was something to do with a prohibition against marking human skin, or perhaps it was a legacy of the concentration camps where numbers were tattooed on inmates' arms. At the time I really had no idea what his problem was.

Occasionally I did try to tell him what my problem was. He would proclaim with total certainty that the world had been created in six days or that the plagues of Egypt occurred exactly as described in the book of Exodus. I couldn't believe that. For some reason it was the plague of darkness that made me speak out. It wasn't that I didn't feel intellectually insulted by the other suggestions. It was just the idea that the whole of Egypt was shrouded in darkness while light shone only on the area in which the Israelites dwelt was just too much, and I said so.

"If you don't believe it, then you're not really Jewish!" he shouted. This was possibly one of the only things he said that I felt able to believe. Perhaps it was in that moment I learned that if religion is a human response to uncertainty, then responding with dogmatic assertions (never mind highly questionable physics) to those who ask questions of it is unlikely to encourage their continued adherence to it. Yet the whole place seemed geared to do that. On Saturdays there were prayers making unreasonable claims about and demands of the Divine Power. On Sundays came stories describing that Power's impossible acts and dubious ethical values. To that was added the impenetrable language that occupied Tuesday and Thursday evenings (and countless hours at home trying to master the learning of the Hebrew portion that was apparently my ticket to Jewish adulthood). All in all the prospects of my one day wearing a badge stating 'Jewish Education Is More Important Than Anything Else' would have seemed ridiculous.

Yet perhaps the seeds of my journey were already being sown. For all my hostility towards it, and apparent rejection of it, my Jewish heritage was being implanted within me. It is not possible to be neutral towards one's religious heritage, especially one with the history and tradition, the triumphs and the tragedies that characterise Judaism's almost four thousand year history. The challenge, I think, is to present it in a way that pays tribute to that heritage, that honours the devotion and commitment of those who cherished and transmitted its values through countless generations. Of course there are many different ways in which this can be achieved. Clearly the environment in which I received my Jewish education, and the manner in which it was presented, did not work for me. It left me bewildered, angry and confused. Nevertheless, in ways I probably didn't sense at the time, it also made me curious, mystified, and unknowingly connected to it.

Maybe that's what I was trying to tell my congregation of soft toys that *Rosh ha-Shanah* afternoon. I certainly like to think that I was in some way highlighting the stuff that wasn't being explained to me, and the stuff that made no sense to me. Perhaps I was seeking to capture and transmit whatever it is that calls to all Jews at certain times of the year and reminds us of a connection to our ancient past, which continues to speak to us. Or maybe I just thought that whatever those Jews tried to do every year in that social hall, and at weekends in their synagogue, I could do better. Whether that goal has been achieved is not for me to judge. There can be little doubt, however, that my Jewish upbringing was affecting me, guiding me unknowingly towards a place where I would one day seek to add my voice to the transmission of that heritage, albeit in a rather different tone from the one in which it was being transmitted to me.

* * * * * * * * * * * * *

This coming Friday is a Jewish holiday. Now before you all reach for your computers to e-mail and tell me that Easter isn't actually a Jewish holiday, let me tell you that it coincides this year with the Jewish festival of Purim.

Purim is a sort of Jewish Red Nose Day - it has associations with the giving of gifts to the needy and also an opportunity for us to dress up and behave ridiculously as we listen to the Book of Esther in synagogues. Indeed according to Jewish tradition, it's compulsory to become so merry that we can no longer distinguish between the villain and hero of the Purim story.

It's the one occasion of the year when Jews are encouraged not to take themselves and their religion seriously. As such, it stands in great contrast to the rest of the year when Judaism reclaims its serious view of the world. Of course this is right and proper: religion is a serious matter and deals with serious and profound issues.

When I first announced to my family that I wanted to become a rabbi, the response from my late grandfather was that I wasn't serious enough to be a rabbi. But with respect to my grandfather, I think the problem lies with Judaism - and religion in general - rather than with me. I actually think that religion is guilty of being too serious, of taking itself too seriously. For me, religion is asking questions about how to do what God wants us to do and trying to find answers to those questions. The problem is that too many religious groups become so convinced that their answers are the only correct ones that they lose sight of what religion is actually for: to help human beings live together in peace and do God's will.

Of course not every day is like this Friday with its fancy costumes and silly behaviour. But Judaism - and all religions - might do well to take some of the humour which will be around for us this weekend and recognise that if we all took our traditions, our religions and ourselves slightly less seriously, we might actually manage to get on a little better. And that, in the end, is what religion is supposed to be about.

(Pause for Thought, BBC Radio 2, 23rd March 2005)

The turning point in my relationship with Judaism would come at summer camp. This is an institution that has found its place in the hearts of many young Jews who have participated in its activities and enjoyed its unique environment. Of course, it doesn't work for all those who take part in the residential experience where an English boarding school temporarily becomes an oasis of Jewish custom and practice for two weeks in the summer. My first summer at camp did little to suggest that I would choose to spend fifteen consecutive years at such an institution as an adult, in a place that would change my life.

When I was just eight years old, some young men came into our Sunday Hebrew class with information about one such camp for children aged nine to fifteen. It started on my ninth birthday so, seeing this as a sort of sign, I persuaded my parents to allow me to experience what would turn out to be probably the loneliest and most miserable two weeks of my life. The camp was run according to strictly Orthodox rules and one of my few memories was of everyone stumbling around in the dark on Friday night as it was forbidden to switch on the lights. One child actually fell down some stairs and broke his arm. This manner of observing the Jewish Sabbath added to my general sense of bewilderment with my Jewish identity. I returned to my synagogue at the age of nine, even more confused, to continue my journey to Jewish adulthood. This would last for four more years before being acknowledged the week after I turned thirteen at the ceremony known as *bar-mitzvah*.

I thought that a *bar-mitzvah* was some kind of ordeal that one had to perform in order to become an adult Jew. That ordeal included chanting some biblical Hebrew in front of the synagogue congregation on a Saturday morning. Like so much of what I was told or shown about my religion in my childhood years, none of this was actually true. A *bar-mitzvah* isn't something you have. It certainly isn't a verb, as in 'I was *bar-mitzvah*ed'. It's actually something you become: a 'son of the commandments'; one who is obliged to observe the instructions and rituals of Judaism. You become it by turning thirteen.

Had I lived several hundred years earlier in one of the many small Jewish communities in Eastern Europe, the significance of becoming *bar-mitzvah* would have been more apparent. In the self-contained world of the *shtetl*, the section of a village or town that was inhabited exclusively by Jews, everything was shaped by Judaism and its culture. Boys were educated in Hebrew and Jewish studies from a very early age. A bright boy might be able to read from the Torah and lead the synagogue service from the age of six or seven. But no matter how bright he was, a boy could not be counted as an adult member of the congregation until he reached the age of thirteen. In the second century of the Common Era, the rabbis decreed that this was the age at which a boy would be sufficiently mature to fulfil his religious obligations. (Incidentally, the rabbis also decided that girls would achieve that same level of maturity at the age of twelve!)

These same rabbis also wanted to emphasise the importance of community. They agreed that certain prayers could take place only if a minimum of ten men were present. The synagogue in which such worship took place was constantly filled with men, young and old, and no one could be sure who was a Jewish adult (i.e. over thirteen) and who was not. In order to save whoever wished to lead a service from having to ask numerous boys whether or not they were thirteen years old, it was agreed that a boy should be called to say the blessing before and after the reading from the Torah on the Sabbath immediately following his thirteenth birthday. This was to indicate to the congregation that this young man could now be counted as part of the necessary quorum of ten men (*minyan*) from then onwards. That was the sole purpose of a *bar-mitzvah* 'ceremony'. The reading of a section of Torah, not to mention the overindulgent celebrations and lavish gifts are a recent, and perhaps not entirely welcome, innovation.

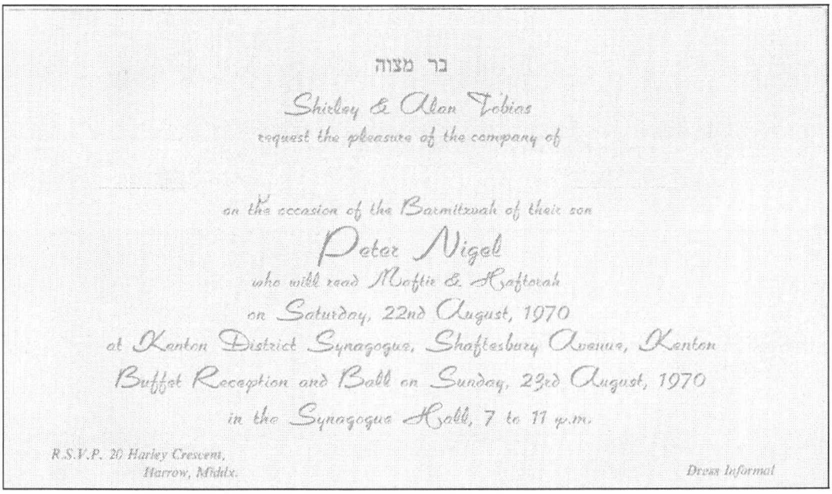
בר מצוה

Shirley & Alan Tobias

request the pleasure of the company of

on the occasion of the Barmitzvah of their son

Peter Nigel

who will read Maftir & Haftorah

on Saturday, 22nd August, 1970

at Kenton District Synagogue, Shaftesbury Avenue, Kenton

Buffet Reception and Ball on Sunday, 23rd August, 1970

in the Synagogue Hall, 7 to 11 p.m.

R.S.V.P. 20 Harley Crescent,
Harrow, Middx.

Dress Informal

The not-entirely-welcome party my parents threw for me took place in the same building that had seen my performance the previous morning, not to mention the years of apparent preparation for it. I had dutifully chanted the final section of the weekly Torah reading *(maftir)* and the section from the Prophets *(haftarah*) in Hebrew, without the faintest idea of the meaning of what I had said. In order for any of that to have happened, one final ordeal, in addition to learning all that Hebrew, had to be overcome. This was something called a '*bar-mitzvah* test'. Every boy wishing to celebrate his *bar-mitzvah* ceremony in a United Synagogue (or rather, every boy whose parents wanted him to do so), had to be examined at the headquarters of that organisation, then in Woburn House in central London.

I recall being seated at a table in a small room opposite an elderly, bearded man. He thrust various books in front of me and asked me to read the contents (all Hebrew) and even to translate some sections. I responded to the man's requests with a stubborn, if somewhat embarrassed, silence. Nevertheless, I was given permission to celebrate my *bar-mitzvah* ceremony a few weeks later. I left there wondering what it would have taken to fail that test. Thinking back to that time, I also wonder what the consequences of failure might have been. Would I have been obliged to remain twelve years old until such time as my Hebrew reached the necessary standard?

The day after I had duly performed the words painstakingly learned by heart without the slightest knowledge of their meaning, I sat in the same building celebrating that event. I was wearing a ridiculous 1970s dress shirt with frilly bits all over it, a source of hilarity to my contemporaries who were taking part in a youth club event elsewhere in the synagogue that evening. I still recall my embarrassment when I encountered a group of them while leading a conga of ageing relatives around the building.

Those same relatives stood with me for the obligatory family photo taken, strangely, in front of the main exit so that the sign 'WAY OUT' stands above this portrait. It may have been a description of the family in the photo, but I prefer to regard it as an opportunity to escape. I needed no second invitation.

* * * * * * * * * * * * *

Why is it that exams always take place at the warmest time of the year, when the heat saps your energy and concentration? It reminds me of a story about a student who was sitting his final exams at a well-established English university. Just after the exam started, he summoned the invigilator and demanded his free pint of beer, as stated in an archaic set of university exam rules he had discovered. After much debate, his pint of beer was begrudgingly delivered. The following day, the same student was summoned to the office of the university chancellor and fined for sitting the exam without wearing a sword...

My thoughts and sympathies go out to all those students taking SATs, GCSEs, 'A' levels and who knows what other tests we put our children through in this summer heat. I don't know about you, Johnnie*, but I have pretty unpleasant memories of my exams. The desperate attempt to remember information, that gut-wrenching feeling that everyone around me knew more than I did. I think that one of the reasons I spent several years teaching before I became a rabbi was to get my own back on a system that seemed determined only to test how much we could remember and regurgitate rather than ascertain what kind of people we were and could become.

In the examination halls across the country, there won't be pints of beer being ordered or swords being worn this summer. But there will be several empty tables that should be occupied by teenagers who have lost their lives in our troubled, violent society. Missing from those tables will be Jimmy Mizen,** and so many other innocent victims like him who could have given so much more to the world than a few correct answers on a piece of paper, who have been let down by a society that seems determined to label people as successes or failures.

I don't know how or even if it's possible to construct exams that offer encouragement and hope to our teenagers. But there seems little doubt that we have to find a way of valuing people based on who they are and what they can become rather than on what they can remember and write down. If we don't, the levels of frustration, disappointment and anger will continue to rise in the summer heat and there will be more pints of beer being ordered and more swords being worn by young people encouraged to regard themselves as failures.

(Pause for Thought, BBC Radio 2, 14th May 2008)

* Johnnie Walker, sitting in for Terry Wogan
** Jimmy Mizen, a sixteen year-old boy murdered in South London, 10th May 2008

That, so I thought, was the end of my relationship with Orthodox Judaism. With hindsight, I now realise that all Jews have some kind of relationship with Orthodox Judaism. Even those who are most determined to reject it end up paying homage to it. I recall being told about the Jewish anarchists in the East End in the 1930s who would stand outside synagogues on Yom Kippur offering bacon sandwiches to hungry worshippers. The choice of the filling was a testimony to the tradition they sought to dismiss and reject. Even Liberal Judaism must inevitably look to the structure and substance of Orthodoxy for its basis, defining itself as much by those elements of tradition it rejects as by its own creativity and innovation.

Not that I knew anything about Liberal Judaism at what I assumed was my point of departure from my religious heritage at the age of thirteen years and seven days. My exposure to the faith of my ancestors had been exclusively in the context of the United Synagogue from which I took my leave, rejecting, so I wrongly believed, all contact with organised religion.

The background music to that rejection came from the pompous lyrics of Greg Lake, accompanied by Keith Emerson's bombastic keyboard playing and Carl Palmer's manic drumming. 'Can you believe/God makes you breathe?' they asked, adding, 'Why did He lose/Six million Jews?'

The absence of God was very much a feature of the early 1970s, not just from my life but, it seemed, from the whole world. British society was being torn apart by industrial disputes that politics was unable to deal with, the focus of international tension switched from Vietnam to the Middle East, and English football was a disaster. None of this was terribly helpful for a teenager being assured by his musical heroes in the same song that dismissed God and religion that he '...must believe in the human race'.

But in that same piece, entitled 'The Only Way', they advised that everyone should seek to make sense of the world in their own way. For this Emerson Lake and Palmer fan, who saw them at his first live concert in 1972 (ticket 75p), that way was not entirely clear. Every Jewish New Year reintroduced me to the Judaism I had sought to reject, and it was in the summer before that concert that I also encountered Judaism's Liberal manifestation for the first time—exactly two years after my *bar-mitzvah* ceremony.

That encounter was another, more successful two week stay at a Jewish summer camp. Given my first experience, the idea of returning to such a place may have seemed inadvisable, but friends of my parents told them of this new venture called *Kadimah* Holiday School which had started in 1971 and they were persuaded to send my sister and me there in the summer of 1972. The Jewish content of this Liberal camp was far less intrusive than had been the case in my previous ordeal. Inevitably there was some religious material, but this proved relatively easy to ignore as my teenage contemporaries and I concentrated on the early 1970s version of trying to be cool.

I spent two summers at *Kadimah* and returned five summers later, a university student en route to becoming a primary school teacher, looking for the chance to develop some teaching skills. There were plenty of opportunities in an environment rich with informal educational possibilities, albeit punctuated by occasional annoying and embarrassing participation in Jewish ritual activities.

Only those who have experienced the unique atmosphere of a Jewish summer camp can properly understand its impact on a participant's identity, attitudes, relationships and development. It offers an escape from the world of everyday into an environment where it is possible to find a lively, mutually supportive community that is dedicated to providing what its organisers believe to be an enriching experience. It didn't work for me at the Orthodox camp when I was nine, but *Kadimah*, the summer school of the Union of Liberal and Progressive Synagogues, most certainly did. It included a dynamic educational theme that was integral to the programme. Without this component, its director once told me, the institution would have no value in his eyes. This was much more than a camp where young people played sport or learned arts and crafts. It was a self-contained world in which moments of Jewish history were brought to life with creativity, humour and love.

One year the theme might be the rabbis who wrote the *Mishnah*, the first compendium of Jewish interpretation, and the school would be transported to Roman times with supervisors dressed in togas and constructing chariots. Another might take us to 18th century Eastern Europe and the world of the *shtetl*, with its *Chasidic* Jews and their traditional beliefs and practices. Or the achievements of the Golden Age of Spain, the ancient world of biblical Israel, or the Babylonian world that produced the giant tome of Jewish law and lore known as the Talmud. Each summer fortnight offered a new educational focus, the opportunity to bring to life the experiences of my ancestors, and the beliefs and traditions that grew from those experiences. Not to mention the chance to dress up in ridiculous costumes.

Of course there was still that religious stuff that had so irritated me during my younger years: daily services, the recitation of Grace after Meals and Sabbath celebrations. Initially I tolerated these as a necessary evil, but slowly I began to appreciate that they were an integral part of each historical experience that was being presented. Here was an opportunity to add depth to that encounter with the past. The prayers and the practices that were present in every Jewish community we visited and recreated served to establish a sense of connection with a Jewish heritage of which there had been not the slightest hint in my earlier experience. We created activities in which groups of young children huddled together in stairwells to recite prayers while trying to evade supervisors playing the role of Inquisitors in fifteenth century Spain or escaped from pogroms in Russia by making imaginary journeys across Europe to find new lives in the West. *Kadimah* brought the Jewish experience of history to life, allowing its participants to establish an emotional connection with their heritage.

The journey from there to becoming a rabbi was a long one. It still seemed improbable that the idea of the Judaism to which I was finally being introduced and with which I was gradually becoming familiar could have any relevance to my life in the 1980s. That selfish, financially obsessed, greedy, Thatcherite world seemed to have no need of, or place for, God or religion either. It was a brutal world in which the poor were becoming poorer and the rich richer; a world in which human aspiration seemed to be limited to the acquisition of possessions, greedily exploiting the weak and vulnerable members of society in that quest.

That was remarkably similar to the world we visited one summer at *Kadimah* that focused on the Prophets of ancient Israel. Amos and Isaiah also lived at a time where society was riddled with inequality. They spoke out against these ills in the name of the God of Israel, bravely criticising the injustices they saw all around them.

The prophetic theme that appealed to me the most was their attack on insincere worship. They lambasted the Israelites who believed that their commitment to their God began and ended with the sacrificial offering they brought to His Temple. Fearlessly they declared that this was not what God wanted, that the music and prayers of their worship would go unheard and that their offerings would be rejected. Time and again they and others repeated their message: this is not a God who demands insincerely offered animal sacrifice. What God wanted was a society in which people would, to use Amos's famous words, '... let justice roll down like waters, righteousness like an everflowing stream'.[4]

Suddenly there was a connection between their era and mine, their lives in the eighth and seventh centuries before the Common Era and mine in the twentieth century of it. Their message, urgently needed and largely ignored in their time, was equally necessary for mine. That summer I heard that message in the prayers and the readings that were incorporated into our creative religious services. I also recognised it in the more formal environment of the Liberal synagogue I subsequently joined. Here was a form of worship that was accessible and rich with meaning and challenge. For so long my ancient faith had confused and bewildered me: here was a version that spoke to me and to the age in which I was living. It embodied the human search for justice and yearning for peace. It presented religion as a reminder of, and a call to, that search. I was moved to add my voice to that timeless call.

* * * * * * * * * * * * *

[4] Amos 5:24

This is the time of year when I always get myself into trouble. You see, Chris, it's the festival of Passover next week, the occasion when we remind ourselves of how our ancestors escaped from slavery in Egypt and of how important it is that we do our best to combat oppression in our world. Like all Jewish festivals, this one is associated with food. But this one is all about food big time. Traditional Judaism demands that any leavened food must not be found within one's home - the biblical book of Exodus actually says within your borders. So it's a massive time for clearing out one's home, and ensuring that any food not specifically kosher for the festival of Passover is nowhere to be seen.

Two and a half thousand years ago the prophet Isaiah stood at the Temple in Jerusalem and watched the people bringing their offerings of lambs and bullocks to sacrifice to God. He ranted at them, complaining that they were just going through the motions of being seen to be doing the right thing, and then they went home and continued exploiting the poor and ignoring the needy in their society. People didn't like to hear this; they preferred to believe that as long as they carried out the rituals of their religion, God would approve of them.

I suppose I like to see myself as a modern version of Isaiah. I think it's my role to shout at all the Jewish people who think that the festival begins and ends with making sure that their homes have nothing in them that breaches the laws of Passover. If I were brave enough, I'd say that if all the rituals and symbols of Passover don't remind us of our ancestors' escape from slavery and encourage us to work to ensure that no one is oppressed anywhere in the world, then they're really just a waste of time.

Like Isaiah in his day, I'll probably get carted away and severely reprimanded for saying such things. So before that happens, let me apologise for having insulted all Jews and extend my observation to insult everyone: I believe all faiths should take a look at their rituals and symbols and ask if they fulfil what I believe to be the basic purpose and obligation of religion: to promote peace and harmony on our fragile planet.

(Pause for Thought, BBC Radio 2, 23rd March 2010)

I have always envied the prophets. That certainty with which they could begin their proclamations 'The word of the Eternal One came to me and said...' and then launch a blistering attack on the social ills of their society. The speeches of Isaiah and Amos were key elements of the Jewish heritage to which I was belatedly introduced. They spoke to the angry teenager who had accompanied me into my twenties and provided a new framework for confronting those aspects of the world of the 1980s that I found so distressing: the inequality and the greed, the hostility and the emptiness. These were elements of human society that inspired the visions and demands of my ancient ancestors. Two and a half thousand years later, little seemed to have changed.

Of course, much had changed. Human civilisation had developed to the point where it no longer saw the vicissitudes of nature as manifestations of divine pleasure or wrath. Shielded and protected from the elements, human beings developed a confidence in their own creations, detaching themselves from a dependence on an invisible external force. Everything could be managed by human action. Society became more sophisticated, but the inequalities that had so outraged the prophets remained. Modern day prophets spoke out against this injustice, but they did so in the name of humanity rather than at the prompting of a divine power. "You shall love your neighbour as you love yourself, I am the Eternal One!" proclaimed the teachers of ancient Israel. "You shall love your neighbour as you love yourself!" echoed their modern descendants, politicians who claim to be fulfilling the prophets' demands while neatly excising the divinely ordained aspect of that obligation.

Of course it made perfect sense to remove God from that equation. This was the age of modernity, where human beings understood their world and could control their own destiny. What did God have to do with it? Perhaps there were occasions on the journey that took me from teacher to studying for the rabbinate when I considered entering the world of politics, the more obvious means by which to introduce change into society.

That didn't happen because I was conscious of a silent prompting, a sense that changing society was actually only part of the challenge. What really needed to change was the attitude and understanding, the perceptions and the awareness of the people in that society. Had I lived two thousand years earlier, I might have been able to stand up and declare that it was God who was suggesting this to me. This was how the prophets had functioned. As they launched into their fearless tirades against the ills of their world, or presented a vision of how they believed that world ought to look, prophets like Hosea or Jeremiah would declare that they were speaking in the name of God. Such a claim had no place in the brutally materialistic world of the 1980s, a world which had departed from God or from which God had been encouraged to depart.

And so the challenge of finding God, or rather a way to rediscover and then reintroduce God, remained. But which God?

Unlike my esteemed ancestors who might experience a mystical encounter in the wilderness, from which they would then emerge to speak in God's name, I had no such basis for my visions and declarations. Indeed, I had been completely bewildered by my childhood introduction to the whole notion of God and His demands. Now that I was in a Liberal environment, Judaism was beginning to make sense. In addition to the powerful visions of the prophets that underpinned Liberal Judaism's religious message, I understood, and benefited from, its emphasis on community. The sense of belonging to a community whose practices and traditions stretched back across the centuries offered a connection with my ancestors who had searched for God, as I was doing now.

Somehow God seemed to have been more available to them, or at least that's how it seemed from the words they wrote, the beliefs they fostered, the certainty with which they practiced their traditions. What, though, had been the result of those words, beliefs and practices? Had the world changed, improved, or risen to the challenge of the God of Israel's prophets? Micah and Isaiah had seen a vision of a world in which all weapons of war would be turned into 'ploughshares and pruning-hooks'.[5] My world was threatening to destroy itself with nuclear weapons. Amos had decried a society in which the poor were purchased for silver, '...the needy for a pair of sandals'.[6] My society was one in which the gap between the rich and the poor continued to grow, which declared that greed was good. If

[5] Micah 4:3; Isaiah 2:4

[6] Amos 8:6

the peace and social justice envisioned by the prophets was indeed the will of God, why was it so frighteningly absent in my time, more than two thousand years after these brave individuals had identified and demanded it?

Once more the words of Emerson Lake and Palmer broke through, challenging me to believe in a God who appeared to have presided over so much prejudice and injustice. This was not the God of justice and harmony, but the one who had failed to prevent the Holocaust and countless other acts of human cruelty that seemed only to amplify God's silence and emphasise God's absence from my world.

Perhaps it was at that point that I heard the echoes of my father's challenges to me - his sarcastic statement on that *Rosh ha-Shanah* morning, congratulating me on having worked out all the answers, his still unanswered question of "What is your understanding of God?".

As I commenced my studies to become a rabbi, I had no more answers than had presented themselves to me in the bathroom scene of ten years earlier. Had my father continued to demand of me an explanation of my understanding of God, I would have presented no certainty, no account of a life-changing vision or dramatic conversion. I might have looked at him and shrugged, admitting that finding proof of a divine presence in a century strewn with apparent evidence of its non-existence was an impossible task. Had I been able to put into words what I now believe was propelling me along that improbable path towards becoming a rabbi, I might have said that the emptiness of the world from which we had driven so many aspects of the Divine made the need to search for God all the more urgent. At that time, though, I did not possess the vocabulary to make such a statement.

The unspoken doubt that still accompanied me as I began my rabbinic studies moves the emphasis in the question 'Why Am I Here?' inexorably to the 'Why?' Why did someone initially so hostile to and dismissive of his religious heritage return to it and, still bearing so many doubts about it and the God in whose name it purported to speak, seek actively to teach and promote it?

THE PRESIDENT, CHAIRMAN AND COUNCIL OF
LEO BAECK COLLEGE
have pleasure in inviting you
to attend the Ordination of

Pauline Bebe, Helen Horn,
Seth Kunin and Pete Tobias
at 3 pm on Sunday
8 July 1990 / 15 Tammuz 5750
at
WEST LONDON SYNAGOGUE
UPPER BERKELEY STREET, LONDON, W1
The Service will be followed by a Reception in the Stern Hall

RSVP by 22 June to
Leo Baeck College
80 East End Road, London N3 2SY
Tel: 081-349 4525

Kindly bring this
invitation with you

As a religious leader, people often expect me to be able to know things about God. After all, isn't that what religion is meant to be about? Well, not really. I think that religion is about trying to understand God - and trying to understand something isn't the same as actually knowing or understanding what that something is.

Religion started as an attempt by human beings to make sense of all the things in their world that didn't make sense. Thousands of years ago, that meant just about everything. And anything that couldn't be explained was placed into the hands of God. God doesn't have hands, of course, but we like to think of God as possessing human characteristics.

But I don't know much about God at all. I don't think anyone does- and I'm always a bit wary about people who say they do - particularly if they say they read it in a book that God wrote.

Whatever else God does - and I happen to think that's quite a lot - I'm pretty sure that doesn't include writing books. People write books. They write books and then, in some cases, claim that God wrote them.

But what these books really contain is human beings writing about what they think God wants. And when those books say things about no one killing anyone else and about the need to establish justice in our societies, it's reasonable to assume that God approves of such books. It's even reasonable to think that God encourages us, in some unfathomable way, to work to introduce such things into our world.

But when those books say things about killing other humans or driving them out of their lands, when followers of religions that have different books bomb and maim and kill one another, I think it's also reasonable to say that this isn't what God wants.

In the end, I'm only guessing. And if God does have hands, I would imagine that right now God's head is buried in those hands, averting tear-stained eyes from the latest scenes of carnage and destruction being carried out apparently in the name of religion.

Religion started as a way of making sense of things that don't make sense. In our modern world, it seems in some cases to have become the cause of them. And not even God could make sense of that.

(Pause for Thought, BBC Radio 2, 19th June 2006)

3. The emphasis on 'Why'

'What does the Eternal One require of you?
Only to do justice and love mercy and walk humbly with your God'
(Micah 6:8)

My past relationship with Judaism meant that my decision to become a rabbi raised a significant number of questions, not to mention eyebrows. After all, as a rabbi I was, in the eyes of many, some kind of 'spokesman for God'. So the first part of the question 'Why?' needed to be addressed to the angry teenager who had sung along defiantly to Emerson Lake and Palmer's rejection of God. After all, it was just over a decade earlier that I couldn't believe He made me breathe...

In my early years as a student rabbi, the oversimplified solutions offered by my 1970s rock heroes haunted me as I attempted to explain my reasons for committing myself to a belief in a divine power. The educational, social justice and community building elements of my chosen path as discovered at *Kadimah* summer camp and in my understanding of Liberal Judaism were relatively easy to rationalise, but the search for a justification of God's presence was as elusive as that presence itself had been on that wet November night on Watford High Street. It seems rather obvious now, but the harder I looked, the more elusive God became.

It was an interfaith event at a church in Birmingham that first afforded me an opportunity to express an understanding of God with which I was comfortable. I was in my first year as a fully qualified rabbi, but my 'L' plates were still firmly attached. I was sitting on a panel with two Christian ministers and we were discussing various aspects of God. I was asked a question from the floor.

'How can you believe in a God that creates babies and Rottweilers?' came the challenge.

I vaguely recall that there had recently been a horrific story of a large dog mauling a baby to death. I don't recall my exact words. In a manner similar to my attempt to answer my father's question several years earlier, I dithered a little and mumbled uncertainly about different elements of creation. Then, with a flash of sudden insight, I pointed out that in addition to creating babies and Rottweilers, God had also given human beings the wisdom to recognise the danger if the two were left together unsupervised. Moreover we had been granted the ability to build cages for violent animals in order to protect vulnerable humans from them.

The answer seemed to satisfy the questioner. I was rather pleased with it as well. It has certainly informed my attempts to understand God's presence in suffering. There are forces in nature - potentially violent animals, earthquakes and hurricanes, cancers and other lethal diseases - that have the capacity to damage and destroy human life. They are built into the fabric of existence alongside the creative forces that sustain us and give us life. My understanding is that God cannot prevent them or interfere in the processes that cause them to occur because that would disrupt the order of the universe. The force to which we give the name 'God' is bound up with, or even part of, nature; it cannot step outside itself and change nature on a whim.

There is something God can do, and does (or, perhaps, this is what God is). Built into human beings is the ability to protect against some (though not all) of the more extreme elements of nature. We can use satellite technology to anticipate the arrival of storms; we can construct buildings in ways that might better enable them to withstand earthquakes – though we can never guarantee that our efforts will suffice to protect us completely. Another element of our humanity is the compassion that is evoked when we witness the suffering of others. It could be argued that this is also a manifestation of the divine in us. Humans regularly demonstrate their ability to care for others, whether it be an immediate response, offering support and shelter to those around us in danger, or charitable contributions following news of a natural disaster.

I think our response to illness is the same. Humanity's determination to overcome its susceptibility to bacteria and viruses is, I believe, another example of something divine that has been implanted within our species. Here, too, we are not always successful, but we can perhaps identify God in the care and attention of so many people dedicated to the preservation of an individual life. In such circumstances God can also be found in our recognition of the impact of that individual's suffering on loved ones who can often do no more than look on helplessly. It is in our caring for one another and our resilience to suffering and misfortune that we find God, not in prayers for miraculous recovery that are as improbable as persuading an angry Rottweiler not to maul a helpless baby. Storms, sickness and road traffic accidents are an inevitability of physics. God resides in our ability to respond to them and, when their consequences threaten to overwhelm us, our capacity to retain hope and dignity in the face of adversity and tragedy.

What of suffering inflicted on people by their fellow human beings? So much of it is carried out ostensibly in the name of a religion, a warped understanding of the Divine. Does not the existence of human barbarity and indifference cry out in denial of God's existence? How can we believe that God makes us breathe if He lost six million Jews, not to mention countless millions of others?

Cruelty is an aspect of human nature, just as tsunamis and cancers are an aspect of physical nature. The difference is that humans have the capacity to choose how they behave. Genuine religion is the attempt to direct that behaviour towards positive, constructive ends; God is the spirit that encourages that effort and yearns for such an outcome. When we fail, God's devastation and dismay at our failure is no less than our own. God didn't lose six million Jews, God didn't cause the deaths of countless innocent victims in wars and genocides. We did. It was our human failure to control our own behaviour, our own nature. That such acts cause most of us to weep shows that we possess a divinely given ability to differentiate between what is wrong and what is right. Maybe, when confronted with this human ability to cause destruction and misery, God weeps also. Perhaps, in the venture we call religion, one of our roles is to try to help wipe away God's tears.

* * * * * * * * * * * * * *

This morning I'd like to consider a religious question... According to author Rabbi Harold Kushner, it's actually the religious question. His book, 'When Bad Things Happen to Good People?' begins like this: 'There is only one religious question: why do innocent people suffer?' All other theological questions, he says, are interesting, but ultimately irrelevant.

Every now and then an event occurs that forces us to ask ourselves such a question. A natural catastrophe, an international outrage or, on a more personal level, an aggressive terminal illness. So many bad things happen in our world, it might sometimes seem that maintaining any belief in God is a futile and forlorn exercise.

But tragedies, whether of natural or human origin, occur because they can occur. Suffering is as much a part of life as joy and it's not reasonable or even fair to expect God to intervene and prevent the catastrophes caused by accidents of nature or the cruelty of human beings. The world, whether it be tectonic plates or tiny cells in our bodies, behave according to certain rules, and God can't change those rules.

But what God can - and I believe does - do is give us the chance to develop ways of coping with those rules. We instinctively know when something cruel has occurred and we rage and protest at the horror and the cruelty of it. We see the devastation that natural catastrophes can wreak and we feel moved to offer our help and support. We strive to cure deadly diseases and, when we cannot, we find ways of easing the pain of those who suffer. And we cope - perhaps with bravery and tenacity like Jane Tomlinson who fought with such determination against her cancer*, perhaps with the silent dignity with which so much untold pain and grief is borne by so many.

Because God also gives us resources that we can draw on to find consolation for ourselves and offer comfort to others. And from that same source, we also discover courage and strength to cope with what sometimes seem insurmountable tragedies. God does not cause this suffering any more than God can prevent it. But God gives us - or perhaps even is - that spirit within us that enables us to resist, recover from and eventually overcome the bad things that happen in our lives and move ourselves and humankind forwards.

(Pause for Thought, BBC Radio 2, 5th September 2007)

* Jane Tomlinson suffered from terminal cancer and made courageous efforts to raise funds even as her health deteriorated. She died, aged 43, on 3rd September 2007.

That explanation of God might work, but how, then, does it justify or allow for religious service? If, as I believe I have already indicated, the belief in God intervening in the physical world to alter the forces of nature is untenable, what then is the purpose of prayer? The rather bizarre activity of attempting to have a conversation with an invisible divine power may have seemed a worthy and even productive activity in a world that believed the divine power could be persuaded to send rain or prevent famine, but how does it fit in our technically sophisticated twenty-first century?

This is a question I ask myself quite frequently in synagogue, but never does it seem more apposite than at the festival of *Sukkot*, Judaism's harvest festival. In ancient Israel (and, come to think of it, in present day Israel too), the pattern of rainfall appears to coincide closely with the needs of an agriculturally based human society. After collecting the harvest at the end of a long hot summer, the farmers of ancient Israel needed a brief period of rain to soften the parched ground. Ideally, this would be followed by another dry period of two or three weeks to enable the seeds for the following year to be sown, after which prolonged rainfall would water those seeds and ensure their growth.

That's pretty much what happens. It is referred to in the book of Deuteronomy as 'the early rain and the late rain'.[7] However,

[7] (Deuteronomy 11:14).

just in case God didn't remember that the rain was supposed to fall at this time, my ancestors engaged in a ritual involving a pointed palm branch, which clearly seems to have been some kind of rainmaking ceremony. Performing such a ritual at the end of the summer in modern Israel may seem a little strange; doing so in the United Kingdom seems decidedly unnecessary. Nevertheless I, along with countless other British Jews, engage in this rainmaking ritual even as the autumn rains are falling. Why do I do this?

Let me be clear. I do not for a moment imagine that I am poking holes in the sky, nor am I influencing whatever Power dwells beyond it to send rain. Perhaps I am reminding myself that my ancestors did indeed believe that they were doing just that. Maybe I, in my cosy, well-insulated, centrally-heated world, might benefit from that reminder of my vulnerability to the forces of nature and the respect, however bizarrely expressed, that my ancestors held for those forces. The ancient Israelite rituals that have been preserved and transmitted to twenty-first century Jews speak of a time when human beings respected their world. Of course, to us their views of how it worked are variously quaint, misguided and just plain wrong, but they reveal a level of appreciation that is significantly lacking from our complacent world view. If, by revisiting a practice introduced and observed by our ancient ancestors, we are able to gain a little insight into the relationship they enjoyed with their world and its Creator, what can be the harm? It might even inspire in us a sense of the appreciation and awe they felt for the powers at work in the world, which we tend to take for granted.

Nevertheless, it cannot be denied that our ancient ancestors genuinely believed that they could communicate with what they perceived to be the power that controlled the forces of nature, whether through sacrifice or words of prayer. They believed they could make requests of or direct gratitude and appreciation to whatever this invisible yet attentive force might be. Atonement for misdeeds was added to the repertoire of communication with the Divine and it became an essential element of ancient prayer. Many centuries later, the call to engage in that aspect of prayer is one that brings the most reluctant Jews back to their heritage each year. Although my experiences of such occasions in my United Synagogue past left me cold and bewildered, my encounter with the Liberal observance of those days was qualitatively different. Instead of seemingly incessant Hebrew chanting, I listened to and joined in with readings in English that challenged me, demanded from me a response. Sometimes the response was emotional, sometimes it was intellectual. It certainly made sense.

Later I learned how Liberal Jewish liturgists had worked hard since the early nineteenth century to remove from the pages of Liberal prayerbooks anything that was deemed theologically unacceptable. The section from Deuteronomy referring to the early and late rains was also excised from the prayer known as the *Sh'ma*; not because Liberal Jews don't believe in rain, but we reject the suggestion, expressed in that passage, that God might withhold it as a form of punishment. Similarly all mention of animal sacrifice in the Temple was removed as, unlike traditional Judaism that yearns for its return, Liberal Judaism considers this an institution consigned to the past.

Liberal Jewish prayer, like Liberal Judaism itself, seeks to find a balance between the ancient insights of Judaism and our modern understanding of the world. If it were to lean towards the latter, our prayerbook would be filled with thoughtful texts about our responsibility to one another and to our planet, but would read more like a philosophical tract or political manifesto setting out a vision for a perfect world. If it leaned too heavily on Jewish tradition, even without the references to animal sacrifice and other theological obscurities, our prayers would be lengthy lists of God's attributes and achievements, interspersed perhaps with our responsibilities and inadequacies. Neither of these options, nor, it might be argued, anything that sits between their extremes, offers a satisfactory reason for engaging in the curious activity of prayer.

Perhaps the issue is not about the content of prayer but rather about the pray-er: the person doing the praying. The world of the twenty-first century moves at a bewilderingly hectic pace, and seems never to stop. In a life governed by deadlines and overloaded with detail, the need to find moments of solace is inversely proportional to the opportunity to do so. If we stop to reflect on our world and our place in it, we need something on which to focus our thoughts. Repeating words written by our ancient poets and dutifully repeated through the generations might help us to find a sense of perspective as well as reminding us of our connection to them. Some of the language may strike us as archaic, naïve or even silly. It is certainly repetitive. For this reason Liberal Judaism seeks to balance the traditional readings with selections from other elements of our tradition that might inspire us, as well as modern writings by Jews and non-Jews that speak more readily to our twenty-first century sensibilities.

It might also be asked why we read prayers in the language of Hebrew if we do not understand their meaning. I recall hearing a story about a man who was a devout Jew, visiting the synagogue every day to take part in the traditional service, reciting all his prayers in Hebrew. In later life he suffered a stroke which disabled the rational side of his brain and, among other things, he completely lost the power of speech. He was still able to recite all the prayers in Hebrew, however, suggesting that the recitation of liturgy in a foreign language is not intended to be understood, but rather it operates on an emotional level, connecting the worshipper with an ancient past and an indefinable deity.

I think that the Liberal version of Jewish prayer is a constant search for a balance between several competing options. Perhaps the search for meaning in prayer is similar to the search for God. References to God's eternal sovereignty, or the suggestion that this guiding power controls the universe, are often impossible to believe or even conceive. Words of prayer are an attempt to define the indefinable, to approach the unapproachable.

I am often asked why or even if I pray. I struggle to answer because the more I try to offer explanations, the more the inadequacy of such explanations becomes apparent. I might respond by asking what is the appropriate vocabulary with which to engage in any kind of dialogue with an invisible God? Then I would suggest that I occasionally have a need for such communication, a desire for the reassurance of such a presence. Sometimes the ritual recitation of ancient words might reveal to me a glimpse of it. On other occasions an insightful modern reading might remind me of my responsibility to the world and its future, inspiring me to work for the benefit of my fellow human beings and future generations unknown. Or perhaps such opportunities might pass me by, leaving me no clearer as to the purpose of prayer.

I suppose my conclusion would be to say that it is important not to give up, to remain open to all possibilities, and to recognise that prayer, like religion itself, embodies the human quest for understanding of ourselves, our world and our purpose. I believe that my connection to that quest underpins my approach to prayer, so it is necessary to consider how the development of Judaism over three millennia speaks to me and inspires me to speak for it.

* * * * * * * * * * * * *

It's a Saturday morning, the Jewish Sabbath and the community is praying together. At the back of the congregation, a little old lady called Sarah is praying fervently. 'Please God,' she whispers in a desperate little voice, 'let me win the lottery tonight. If I win, then I promise I'll believe in your power from now on.'

A week later, she's there again. 'I asked you last week to let me win the lottery,' she said in her prayer. 'And I didn't. Please let me win the lottery tonight.' Every week, Sarah goes along to the synagogue and prays that she'll win the lottery. And a week later she's always there again, getting increasingly desperate and angry as she asks God to answer her prayer.

Many weeks later, she is finally running out of patience. 'Look God,' she says angrily. 'Every week I pray that you'll let me win the lottery. It's been weeks now and still I haven't won. I don't think I believe in you any more. If I don't win the lottery tonight, I'm never coming back to synagogue again.'

And God, having listened every week to Sarah's prayer, decides that it's time to answer her. A divine voice finds its way to Sarah and says: 'Sarah, do me a favour. Give me a chance here and meet me halfway. Buy a lottery ticket.'

Often in times of difficulty or danger, our thoughts turn towards God and we cry out for help. There are moments in our lives which seem to defy explanation, where we seek answers and that's when, often despite ourselves, we look to some invisible, divine force. In my experience as a rabbi, even the most fervent non-believers find themselves asking questions of God at times of crisis and wondering why they don't seem to be receiving an answer.

Like little old Sarah, they're asking just a bit much of God. You can't win the lottery if you don't buy a ticket. And you can't really expect to find explanations or comfort from religion unless you spend a little time making some kind of investment in the religious process.

But it's easy to become disheartened in prayer. I remember reading an Enid Blyton book in my childhood where the good Christian children were trying to explain prayer to the not-so-good not Christian children. One of the not-so-good Christian children complained that God didn't listen to his prayer. 'In our geography test I wrote down that Paris was the capital of Spain,' he said. 'I realised afterwards that I was wrong, so I prayed to God to make Paris the capital of Spain. And he didn't.'

Praying is a peculiar activity. You might even say it's a bit of a lottery. The secret, I suppose, is to be realistic in what we're praying for. We can't ask God to change the world. But we can ask for help in coping with whatever the world throws at us. And maybe that expectation is the ticket to successful prayer.

(BBC Radio 2, 22nd September 2003)

The religion of Judaism is based on and grounded in the Torah, the Five Books of Moses. Those responsible for my Jewish upbringing tried to persuade me it had been written by God and that it was ostensibly the basis of every Jewish law and custom. I had dared to challenge and question this.

My studies as I trained for the rabbinate confirmed my childhood belief that this book was not divinely authored and therefore was almost certainly not the infallible, unchanging and unchangeable word of God. There are plenty of scholarly theories that confirm what my twelve year-old mind suspected: that the Torah is a document written by human beings. As such it's filled with inaccuracies, contradictions, repetitions and exaggerations, not to mention violence and cruelty. So how could I justify studying it, teaching about it and reading from it in a context that was supposedly sacred?

Actually, that's one of the easier 'why' questions to deal with. For me, releasing the Torah from the straitjacket of divine authorship actually increases its value. Instead of claiming that it is a God-given blueprint for humankind and, in particular, the Jewish branch, my approach to the Torah is to explain that it is a record of my ancestors' quest to discover meaning and purpose in their lives, to impose a social, moral, theological and political structure onto a world that to their eyes could often be chaotic and frightening. Some of their ideas were clearly products of and limited to the time and place from which they emerged. Others are timeless and still speak to our sophisticated but no less frightening society.

The secret of how to approach the Torah is, I think, not to look to it for answers but to look at its laws, rituals and systems of belief and consider what were the situations they sought to address. The sacrifice of animals, for example, was clearly a major feature of my ancestors' relationship with God. The question to ask is not 'Why does God want human beings to offer sacrifices?' but rather 'What were my ancestors of three thousand years ago trying to achieve through animal sacrifice?' The answer ought to suggest that the giving back to God in ritual form of a portion of what God had given them implies a level of respect and gratitude to the Creator. The question then becomes whether sacrifice is any longer an appropriate way to express that respect or the twenty-first century needs to find other ways of acknowledging and demonstrating, recapturing even, that awareness of God.

The narratives of the Torah need also to be treated with caution. These are stories designed to give substance to the identity of a group of people exiled in Babylon, far from their home in the sixth century before the Common Era. There is probably a kernel of truth at the heart of these tales, such as the exodus from Egypt, but several centuries passed between the story first being told and its finally being written down. The final version contained the results of several hundred years of storytelling expertise. Again what matters is the principle. This is a narrative about liberation from slavery, and the fact that the Torah regularly reminds its readers that we were slaves in Egypt and should, therefore, not oppress others, should be regarded as more significant than the story that relays that message.

There are many more examples of the multiple layers of human authorship of the Torah, but space does not permit a full analysis of them here. More worthy of consideration is the way that the Torah moved from being a human account of a people's history, traditions, laws and theology to its current place in Orthodox thinking as a divinely written set of instructions for the fulfilment of God's will to be carried out by that people's descendants.

Nowhere in the Torah is there a claim that its entire contents were written or dictated by God. As I have indicated, my studies have convinced me that it is a compilation of legend and folklore written several centuries after the events being retold actually took place, combined with ancient rules for worship and the establishment of a just society as envisaged by people living almost three thousand years ago. It became the basis of the society that was constructed by the people of Judah who returned from exile in Babylon in the fifth century BCE, but the idea that it had divine authorship was not adopted until the time of the rabbis of two thousand years ago.

The rabbis were one faction of several vying for supremacy in Roman-occupied Judea (the Roman name for what had previously been Judah). Their role was to emphasise the importance of the Torah as the central document underpinning Jewish society and the people's way of life. Other major groups were the Sadducees (the Temple priests) and the Zealots, military fanatics determined to overthrow the Romans. Each group needed a basis on which to establish its authority. The power of the Sadducees was based exclusively on their role in the second Jerusalem Temple. Once it was destroyed by the Romans in the year 70 CE, their power base was gone. When the resistance of the Zealots was finally broken at Masada three years later, they too were removed from the scene. That left only the rabbis, guardians of a book that told the story of how their ancestors developed their relationship with God. Under rabbinic guidance, the approach to that book changed, and it became the basis of God's expectations of the descendants of those ancient Israelites.

The consequences of this were enormous. It meant that Judaism was able to survive the destruction of the second Temple in the year 70. But at the core of that survival was a six hundred year-old document compiled from various sources at a critical moment in Israelite history. Its role then was to provide Judah's exiles with a sense of who they were, what they believed and why their precious city, Jerusalem, had been destroyed by the Babylonians. When the Romans meted out that treatment to Jerusalem a second time, the Torah, as it had now become, served a similar purpose, but for the reasons listed above, it was now invested with divine authority. Moreover, the rabbis claimed that their interpretations of that book also carried equal authority, so that every instruction became a commandment *(mitzvah)*, every prohibition an act to be avoided for fear of angering God.

This was the Judaism that emerged from the catastrophe of Roman domination and repression. It reflected the beliefs and interpretations of one particular group, the only group to survive Roman brutality. For the rabbis of the time, this was no accident. Rather, they saw the survival of their version of Judaism as a manifestation of the Divine will, and considered it their duty to carry forward that will. The customs and practices the rabbis developed were designed either to implement the instructions they identified in the Torah or to prevent their flock from breaking any of the commandments contained within it. Subsequent centuries saw the emergence of rituals and observances, customs and laws that drew their authority from instructions or incidents that were to be found in this revered ancient document.

Judaism thus became a series of obligations and prohibitions based on two thousand year-old interpretations of three thousand year-old laws and customs rooted in an ancient Near Eastern land. Rituals were developed, aimed at enacting those laws. These rituals, and the explanations underpinning them, also assumed the mantle of divine authority. So kindling lights to welcome Shabbat, for example, became a *mitzvah*, a divine commandment, preceded by the blessing assuring candlelighters that what they were doing was commanded by God.

This presents a huge challenge to a Liberal Jew. The lighting of Sabbath candles a prescribed number of minutes before sunset on a Friday is quite clearly not a divine commandment. So why do it - either at the appointed time or at any other time on the eve of the Sabbath? What about all the rituals and prohibitions that attach to the twenty-four hours that follow, each bearing the same assumed divine weight? This, I think, is the biggest question for Liberal Judaism and this Liberal rabbi: why do all this stuff, preceded by words that testify to our acceptance of its divine origin, if we don't believe that God commands us to do so? And if this question cannot be met with a rational, sound response, then the 'why?' of this work's title will remain unanswered.

* * * * * * * * * * * * *

Today I'd like to introduce listeners to an old rabbi - one who lived more than two thousand years ago. His name was Hillel and he said a lot of very wise things.

It was Hillel who came up with what he called the 'Golden Rule' of Judaism: 'Whatever is hateful to you,' he said, 'do not do to a fellow human being.' Some commentators thought that his rule was a bit negative; that the more positive way to express that requirement for ethical and compassionate behaviour between human beings was the verse from Leviticus: 'You shall love your neighbour as you love yourself.'

That's a brilliant law, of course, and I can't help but be impressed that my biblical ancestors came up with such a concept at a time when neighbours in the ancient world were happily beating each other up on a regular basis.

But there's a bit of a problem being told to love someone as you love yourself. Loving yourself is actually something that's very difficult to define. We are so often self-critical, or we feel inadequate in some way or other. I don't want to get too psycho-babbly at this hour on a Friday morning, but maybe the fact that we don't love ourselves properly or enough is partly to blame for the fact that we don't treat other people as well as we might.

But that's enough amateur psychology for one morning. The point is that Hillel got it right. The best way to ensure that there is humane and compassionate behaviour between people is not to do to someone else anything that you would not want done to yourself. It's obvious. No one wants to be mistreated or abused or hurt. So before you say or do something hurtful to another person, stop and ask yourself how you would feel if someone did that to you. Chances are, if you're honest, you'll admit that it would make you feel pretty bad. So why inflict that on someone else?

If we all stuck to that simple rule, then the world really would be a better place and - who knows - we might even end up loving ourselves a bit more as well.

(BBC Radio 2, Pause for Thought, 25th June 2010)

I think the answer to the question 'Why am I here?' lies in the relationship between me and my ancestors. I don't believe that the world was made in six days, but I still read it from the Torah and declare that it is a teaching of righteousness and truth. I know that God did not specifically command me to light Sabbath candles or wave palm branches, but I still carry out the actions and precede them with words saying I am following divine instructions. Perhaps I do this to acknowledge the efforts my ancestors made, in recognition of the beliefs they cherished and the laws and customs they developed to embody and express those beliefs.

As a Liberal Jew, I may choose to omit those elements that offend my twenty-first century logic. Or I may choose to incorporate them, knowing that they represent not a divine demand but my ancestors' striving for understanding and meaning. That choice is the privilege of being liberal. Of course a certain amount of consensus is required for any element of Judaism that is to be observed in a communal setting. But I also reserve the right - indeed, I demand it - to change aspects of my ancestors' belief system and its practices that I consider to be inhumane or unjust. That is the responsibility of being liberal. Liberal Judaism's readiness to re-evaluate Jewish traditions should be based always on the principle of informed choice. This means having an awareness of the underlying reason for a particular ritual or practice set against practical considerations regarding its suitability for or relevance in a modern context.

Instead of revering earlier decisions and surrounding them with an impenetrable protective barrier, we should regard past developments as I believe each generation of our ancient ancestors regarded them. For them they were a starting point, a system designed to address a particular social, political, religious and moral climate at a given time and in a given place. One generation of rabbis made decisions and interpretations in response to the prevailing climate, knowing the inevitability of change since they had already adapted what their predecessors had established. They knew also that the Judaism they introduced would change also, leaving behind old certainties as the discoveries of each new age cast doubt upon them, offering new challenges in their place.

The prophets of ancient Israel had already recognised this centuries earlier. Isaiah and Amos criticised worship that was just for show, reminding the Israelites that God demanded justice, not sacrifice; righteousness, not prayers. For them, making ritually correct offerings or uttering the right words and then continuing to tolerate or even foster a society riddled with injustice was worse than not sacrificing or praying at all. They weren't opposed to worship, just to insincere worship. And a twenty-first century Liberal attitude to prayer and ritual should reflect that same distinction.

Consider these elements of what might be a typical Friday night for me. I praise God by whose commandments I am sanctified and who has enjoined me to light Sabbath candles, then do so, even though the sun set several hours earlier. I carry out this ritual surrounded by electric light and then turn on a cooker to make my Friday evening meal and watch TV afterwards. Is there something wrong with this in the context of traditional Sabbath laws? Some would say that there is, that this is sacrilegious and hypocritical. According to Jewish law, lighting a fire and using electrical items after sunset on a Friday is a breach of the laws of the Torah, an affront to the God whose commandments are contained in that book. For me, the God who might be insulted by such acts is the God of the Creme Egg: the one who sits in judgment, measuring our behaviour against a checklist to be assessed every *Yom Kippur*.

What about someone who observes every Sabbath instruction to the letter, from sunset on Friday until sunset on Saturday, then spends the working week running a business that exploits the less well off members of society, who neglects or mistreats other members of their household, who does not speak out against injustice when the opportunity to do so presents itself? This, surely, is the real affront to God.

Worship and ritual are designed for the person who is worshipping. God has no need of my words or my moments of religious devotion. I do. I perform them for myself, to remind myself of my obligations to whatever it is in, around or beyond me that I call divine. And those obligations are, quite simply, to be, despite my failings, the person I can be. To help to construct, against a background of human selfishness and greed, a society that respects all and that offers support and compassion to all its members. To strive, from a body that is rooted to the earth and confounded by countless physical demands and restrictions, to reach for the stars, to discover purpose, and to fill my life with meaning.

That's what my ancestors did. They did it in a context very different from mine: less knowledgeable perhaps, but almost certainly more humble. If their words, their concepts, their beliefs seem to me archaic and out of date, then I must try to value them not for their content but for what they represent: a genuine search for meaning and understanding, and a recognition, however expressed or demonstrated, of a desire to understand the will of God and to enact that will in their lives and their world. My world may believe it has a greater intellectual and scientific awareness, allowing me to understand the flaws in their logic or their physics, but what matters is the yearning that drove them to reach their conclusions, not the conclusions themselves. I strive to embrace elements of my heritage with that same yearning. They are symbols of the human quest for knowledge and understanding, not, as some might have me believe, divinely ordained instructions to be dutifully observed, which I ignore at my peril. Of course human ethical awareness has also developed and needs to be consulted and incorporated into what is called religion.

This surely is the role of religion: to encourage people to consider their potential, to remind them of their duty to fulfil that potential and to strive to do so in the context of the time and place in which they live, and with whatever resources they have at their disposal. The dedication and quest of those who lived in a time and place different from mine should be added to the knowledge and wisdom of my age. In this social and historical context I read my ancestors' words, grapple with my ancestors' concepts and engage in my ancestors' rituals. When I do this I am not seeking to fulfil an obscure divine commandment. Rather I am engaging in an attempt to discover the devotion, commitment and struggle of my fellow Jews from earlier times, and, in so doing, open up the possibility of experiencing it myself.

* * * * * * * * * * * * *

Two weddings and a bar-mitzvah. This could be a title for a Jewish version of a well-known film but it is in fact just a list of the services which have taken place in my synagogue during the past seven days. To these ceremonies I welcomed a variety of visitors and guests, many of whom were visiting a synagogue for the first time.

On such occasions, I make it my business to ensure that our customs and practices are explained to those who are unfamiliar with them. We also have a day every month when classes of schoolchildren are invited to visit the Synagogue and have the opportunity to hear an explanation of Judaism and to see close up the artefacts and symbols of Jewish tradition.

There is, of course, something slightly artificial about presenting one's religion in such a way. Religion is, at its heart, an expression of an individual's relationship with God, so the public portrayal and explanation of religious beliefs and symbols could perhaps be seen as an intrusion. One's religion is, after all, one of the things about which it is deemed impolite to make conversation.

Such lack of conversation, such lack of communication in the past has led to conflicts which still smoulder in our present day and which occasionally flare up into violent confrontation. One need only look at events in Northern Ireland to see the violence which can emerge when fiercely held religious views are aired in public. And in so many places of the world, battle lines between and within communities are drawn on the basis of differing beliefs or practices which are never properly explained, never clearly understood.

These deeply entrenched misunderstandings of other people's beliefs extend to mistrust of the people themselves. This, in turn, is expressed in hostility and violence. That is why I am so delighted to have been able to welcome so many visitors to my synagogue in recent days. As well as allowing celebrations to be shared, it also raises levels of understanding. And where there is understanding, there will also be tolerance. And where there is tolerance, people will not march senselessly around others' religious institutions shouting insults and brandishing banners of hate, but will enter in and join in celebration.

Thought for the Day, BBC Radio Scotland, 7th July 2000

So why am I here? Why am I in the pulpit as a rabbi, where I have spent the last two decades and more? Being a rabbi is a privilege and an honour, and I begin to understand why, despite all my doubts and hostility towards the religion I profess to represent, I have chosen to be here. Even in moments when I feel angered or insulted by elements of my heritage, or simply unable to connect with it, I recognise the debt I owe to it and the dedication and commitment it has evoked and inspired through the ages. No matter how great my frustration, I feel reassured by an invisible link to co-religionists in nineteenth century Germany, fifteenth century Spain, twelfth century England, fourth century Babylon, first century Judea or that same country, in which my heritage was founded, at any number of times in the thousand years before that date. That connection isn't necessarily with the influential, epoch-making leaders and thinkers of those times and places, but rather with the ordinary Jews who struggled to make sense of their lives and their world and found comfort and consolation, guidance and explanation in their Jewish faith.

And I am humbled, terrified even, by the assumptions that their descendants, members of my community, make about me, my connection with and understanding of that past. In earlier times my role as a rabbi would have been clearer, more easily defined. Jews, and even non-Jews, would have come to me with their questions about aspects of Jewish observance and I would have provided them with answers based on definitive responses by earlier scholars with wisdom and knowledge greater than mine.

But this is a different age: the questions are different, the answers more so. Yet the expectations are similar. rabbis are supposed to provide answers. I am often asked, even by my Liberal congregants, for specific instructions relating to Jewish law—and even, on occasion, to say a prayer during the course of a service for someone's ill or dying relative.

The thought that I am somehow perceived as having that kind of connection with the Almighty is alarming, partly because of what it seems to demand of me, but mainly because of what it says about my congregants' assumptions and expectations of God. While I often feel troubled by some of the questions to which I am expected to have answers, I am more concerned about the ones apparently being posed to God. Such questions seem to be directed to the absent God of Watford High Street or of the Creme Egg. God doesn't work like that, and thoughtful twenty-first century Liberal Jews should know better than to think in such terms.

Religion isn't about what we want, expect or demand of God. It's about what God wants, expects and demands of us. The awareness to which Liberal Judaism, indeed any liberal approach to religion, points is that this clearly does not require slavish adherence to ritual or the literal interpretation of ancient texts. What God demands is that human beings use their intelligence and skill to fulfil their human potential to face and overcome the challenges that life on this planet poses to them. In earliest times of human development, those challenges were about everyday survival in a hostile environment. The belief systems constructed to explain and meet those challenges were similarly simple. In our more sophisticated age, where we know more about that environment and are able in so many ways to manage it, the challenges are more subtle but no less urgent, and our responses to them need to show similar awareness and development. Having gained significant control over our environment, we must learn to manage properly the precious resources of our planet. Having developed sophisticated technology to defend ourselves against the callous cruelty of nature in its physical and human manifestations, we must learn to use it for peaceful ends. Having learned the art of communication, from the earliest alphabets to e-mail, we must learn to share it to establish peace and justice throughout our dangerously divided world.

This is what God commands human beings to do. Religious rituals and symbols are intended to remind us of that divine obligation. I thank God who commands me to light the Sabbath candles and then do so, not because God wants candles lit in my and a few million other homes at a certain time every week, but because God wants me, and all people, to use such symbols as a reminder of my privilege, which is to be alive, and my responsibility, which is to use my life to fulfil God's purpose in bringing justice and harmony to that life and the world in which I live it. I praise God who commands us to shake a palm branch in the autumn and then do so, not because God is carefully counting the number of palm branches being waved in order to decide whether or not to send rain, but to remind myself of my dependence on nature and my responsibility, that of my community and of all humanity, to manage its resources properly.

Rituals and symbols are reminders of God's commandments, not manifestations of them. Religion is the human venture to express those reminders, to symbolise God's demands of humankind, and to make known the responsibility humans have to fulfil those demands. That was the purpose of ancient sacrifice, as the prophets sought to remind our biblical ancestors, that is the purpose of prayer, as the rabbis who composed Judaism's liturgies understood.

When the rabbis of two thousand years ago introduced the idea that rituals were *mitzvot* (divine commandments), they suggested that Jews should precede the carrying out of a *mitzvah* with a formula implying that God had singled them out for this particular task and demanded that they carry it out. Whether this was their genuine belief or part of their attempt to assert their authority is not for me to say. It worked for them;

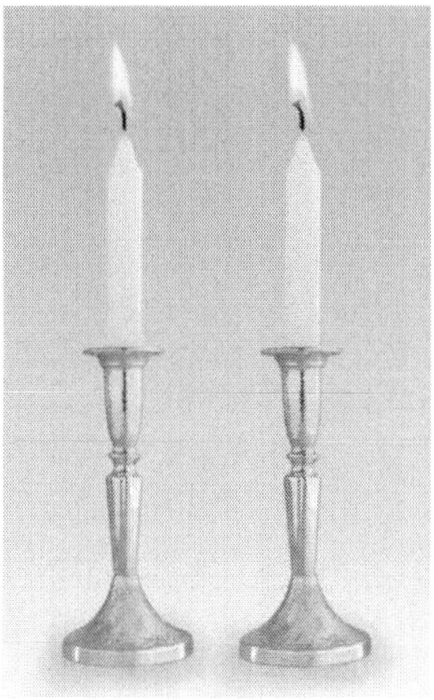

perhaps it still rings true for many modern Jews. I prefer to translate their phrase 'You sanctified us by your commandments and enjoined us to kindle the Sabbath lights', for example, as 'Every human being has a special responsibility to behave in a certain way and this ancient ritual is intended to remind us of that.' For me this offers a glimpse of the purpose of modern worship and religious practice: by drawing on those centuries of yearning, expressed in ancient words and rituals, I am striving to connect with my ancestors' awareness of their relationship with and responsibility to God, and the divine demands placed on them to appreciate, to learn and to grow, and thereby continue to develop that appreciation, learning and growth.

Being a rabbi, being part of that process to foster and to encourage that yearning, for myself and those who are searching with me, offers an answer to the 'why' of my question.

* * * * * * * * * * * * *

Rabbi Hillel used to say 'If I am not for myself, then who is for me? And if I am only for myself, then what am I? And if not now, when?'

Now there's a curious set of thoughts for a Monday morning. Words uttered two thousand years ago by one of Judaism's best known ancient rabbis. 'If I am not for myself, then who is for me?' With these words Hillel reminds us that our prime duty as individuals, as creations of the one God, is to ourselves.

I am reminded of these words when I am sitting on a plane, listening to the safety instructions being uttered by the cabin crew.

'If there is a loss of air pressure in the cabin,' they say, 'oxygen masks will drop from above.' The details of how to fit the mask are then followed by the instruction to attend to your own mask before assisting anyone else. So there's Hillel's point. Make sure you look after your own needs because, in the end, we all have to take responsibility for ourselves.

But having assured our own oxygen supply, then what? Is it sufficient simply to sit back? No. Because if we are only for ourselves, then what are we? If we are in comfort and safety then we have a duty to ensure that everything possible is being done for the comfort and safety of those around us, both in our immediate vicinity and in our fragile world. To ignore this responsibility would be to negate our very humanity.

'And if not now, when?' Any delay in accepting this responsibility and acting upon it can only cause misery and harm. There is good that we can do, hurt that we can mend, now - today - though our own words and actions.

Teach us, Eternal God, to value and look after ourselves, and to recognise what good we can bring into the lives of those around us. Help us this and every day to what is best in Your sight for ourselves and for others. Amen.

(Prayer for the Day, BBC Radio 4, 5th February 2002)

The emphasis on 'Am'

God said to Moses, "I am who I am.
This is what you are to say to the Israelites:
'I am has sent me to you.'" **(Exodus 3:14)**

As the laughter died down in the Biblical Hebrew class following my comment about the emphasis on 'here' in the teacher's 'Why am I here?' question, one of my classmates tried to upstage my witticism by saying, 'And if the emphasis is on 'am', it's a grammatical statement.' It was pretty lame.

In the context of this work, in which a Liberal rabbi seeks to explain the motivation behind his chosen vocation, perhaps it does have a place, albeit at the very end. 'Am' is the present tense of the verb 'to be'. First person singular, to be precise. And it calls to mind the famous maxim of Rabbi Hillel which features in the radio script that precedes this chapter.

My journey through Judaism was and will continue to be largely based around a struggle with big ideas and concepts, historical moments and prophetic insights. My life and work as a congregational rabbi, however, tends only rarely to focus on these ultimate questions. Because although religion claims to be (and sometimes even is) about abstract concepts and critical questions, it's really about people.

Of course it is an honour to be able to represent a religious heritage that is more than three thousand years old and to be able to claim to be standing on the shoulders of Israel's prophets. The real privilege, however, is to be able to play a part in the lives of individual members of a Jewish community.

I would be the first to concede that a major part of the attraction of the rabbinate is the opportunity it offers to be a performer. Many rabbis, I am sure, are would-be actors who love the opportunity to play to an audience. With that opportunity comes responsibility. The true value, I think, of rabbinic work is the chance to accompany people as they confront challenges and questions about their existence at key stages of their lives such as birth, coming of age, marriage and bereavement. These are situations that humans have faced for countless generations and despite our growth in knowledge and understanding, they still speak of a mystery which it is the role of religion to address.

Perhaps that's what religion is really for. Yes, it's there to answer life's big questions, strive for the improvement of humankind, provide a framework for individuals and communities to establish a relationship with an unfathomable creative power that is greater than themselves. All that, and a reminder of our obligation to work to bring justice into our world. Its greatest contribution is that it offers a context within which people can celebrate their special moments and a place to which they can turn when tragedy and sorrow strike.

So the emphasis is on the present - the here and now, the everyday opportunities we have to share aspects of our lives with one another. To be the community that offers support to the individual in need—and occasionally to be the individual who needs the support of the community. It is in supporting and caring, in needing and being needed that we truly fulfil the potential that has been implanted within us.

In the end, the question isn't an existential one, nor an ontological one, nor even a geographical one. It's not really a grammatical one either, not directly anyway. But the 'am' of 'Why am I here?' is about being in the present tense, recognising that for all its focus on the past and its vision for the future, Judaism, or any religion, is about the here and now.

Within the here and now there are so many opportunities to discover what is precious in life. Watching children grow, celebrating turning points in their development with life-cycle events, sharing their and their parents' joys and being with those individuals and families in times of stress, torment and grief. These are some of the privileges of being the rabbi of a congregation. Being able to offer and to oversee a community within which all these moments can be marked, to provide a space in which individuals can feel valued and supported, encouraged and cared for is, I believe, the true expression of our humanity. Life in the present tense, religion focused not so much on the universe and its eternal questions but rather on individuals and their immediate needs. This, I think, is where we truly find God. This is how we learn to value our lives. Here, in the life of my community, is where I find the best explanation for why I am here - with the emphasis on here.

GLOSSARY

This glossary gives brief outline details of some of the words and concepts mentioned in this book which may be unfamiliar to non-Jewish readers. For further information about Judaism, and in particular ~~Liberal Judaism, see~~ my book 'Liberal Judaism: A Judaism for the Twenty-First Century' (Liberal Judaism, 2007)

Amos	Biblical prophet, 8th century BCE
Animal sacrifice	The biblical form of worship practised in many places in ancient Israel before being centralised in the Temple in Jerusalem.
BCE	Before the Common Era; equivalent of BC
CE	Common Era; equivalent of AD
Chasidic	A group of ultra-Orthodox Jews
Elohist ('E')	One of the sources at the heart of the Documentary Hypothesis of biblical criticism; in addition to 'E' there is the *Yahwist* source ('J'), the Priestly source ('P') and the Deuteronomist ('D')
Grace After Meals	A series of blessings traditionally recited after food
Haftarah	A reading from the Prophetic books of the Hebrew Bible, appended to the Torah reading in synagogue on a Sabbath morning
Hebrew Bible	Incorrectly equated with the Old Testament: there are several significant differences between the Christian version of the Bible and the Hebrew Bible, made up of three sections: *Torah* (the Five Books of Moses), *N'vi'im* (the 'Historical' books and the Prophets and *K'tuvim*. (the Writings)
Hebrew Union College	The rabbinical school of the Union of Reform Judaism which has sites in Cincinatti, Jerusalem, Los Angeles and New York
Intifada	Palestinian rebellion against Israeli occupation
Isaiah	Biblical prophet, 8th and 7th century BCE
Israelite	Name given to an inhabitant of biblical Israel
Jeremiah	Biblical prophet, 7th and 6th century BCE

Judah	Southern Kingdom, of which Jerusalem is the centre, the kingdom ruled over by descendants of King David between the 9th and 6th centuries BCE
Kol Nidre	Name given to the service held on the evening of *Yom Kippur*
Kosher	Literally 'fit' - usually referring to food that meets the requirements of Jewish dietary laws
Leo Baeck College	The rabbinical school of the non-Orthodox movements in the UK, named after Rabbi Leo Baeck, a Holocaust survivor, teacher and scholar
Levitical	Relating to the biblical priests, who were members of the tribe of Levi, known as Levites
Liberal Judaism	The movement, founded in 1902, that represents and promotes the liberal aspects of Judaism
Maftir	The concluding section of the weekly Sabbath Torah reading, traditionally divided into seven sections
Minyan	A quorum of ten men over the age of 13 required for certain prayers to be read and rituals to be performed
Mishnah	The compilation of rabbinic decisions gathered together at the end of the 2nd Century CE
Mitzvah (pl. Mitzvot)	Divine commandment(s)
Orthodox	The adjective that describes those Jews who adhere to the traditional Jewish belief that all Judaism stems from the Torah, which was given to Moses at Mount Sinai and can never be changed
Passover (Heb. *Pesach*)	The Jewish spring festival, which also commemorates the Exodus from Egypt
Pogrom	Russian word. Violent mob attack on minority group, historically, though not exclusively, Jewish
Progressive Judaism	Any form of Judaism that is not Orthodox; that believes that the Torah is to some extent a human document

Rabbi	Literally 'my teacher' - the title given to Jewish communal leaders and teachers who have achieved an appropriate academic qualification
Rosh ha-Shanah	The Jewish New Year, which falls in the autumn; ten days before *Yom Kippur*
Sabbath	The seventh day, traditionally a day of rest. Commences at sunset on Friday and ends at sunset on Saturday. According to a literal interpretation of the Torah, this is a day that has many restrictions; a liberal interpretation would emphasise the need for spiritual refreshment on this day of rest
Sadducees	The priests of the second Jerusalem Temple
Shabbat	The Hebrew word for Sabbath
Shavu'ot	The Festival of Weeks; originally celebrating the barley harvest, seven weeks and one day after the second day of Passover
Sh'ma	A reading from the book of Deuteronomy (chapter 6, verses 4-9) which is the statement of Jewish belief in One God
Shtetl	Literally 'little city' (Yiddish) - the Jewish quarter of a town or village in Eastern Europe
Shul	Yiddish word for synagogue
Sukkot	The harvest Festival, takes place two weeks after *Rosh ha-Shanah*
Tallit	A prayer shawl with fringes, traditionally worn by Jewish men in religious services
Talmud	A collection of Jewish opinion, based on the writings in the *Mishnah* and supplemented over many centuries of discussion, particularly in Babylon in the 3rd-6th centuries CE
Temple	The location in Jerusalem, initially built by King Solomon (c 950BCE) and rebuilt after the return from exile in Babylon in the 4th century BCE, finally destroyed by the Romans in 70 CE
Torah	The first five books of the Hebrew Bible and the Christian Old Testament, referred to in Jewish tradition as the Five Books of Moses

United Synagogue	The organisation that oversees mainstream Orthodox Judaism in the United Kingdom and the Commonwealth
Yom Kippur	The Day of Atonement; the tenth day of the Jewish New Year. A day of fasting and prayer from sunset to sunset
Zealots	Military groups of Jews committed to overthrowing the Romans in the first century CE